Very Pretty P[...]
PERMIAN NATIONS

Written by **Evey Lockhart**.
Art by **Sam Mameli, Evlyn Moreau & Evey Lockhart**.
Editing & Development by **Jarrett Crader**.
Development & Design by **Christian Kessler**.
Layout by **David N. Wilkie**.
Proofreading by **Jarrett Crader**.
Playtesters: **Jared Sinclair , Nik, Max, Chase, Reilly & Omar.**

Contents

Overview

Very Pretty Paleozoic Pals: Permian Nations is a setting, or Sphere, for the ***Troika! RPG***, featuring an incredibly ancient and positively adorable fantasy land. Before even the existence of dinosaurs:

- Fabulous Dimetrodons defined wetland fashion.
- Behorned Xenacanthus sharks deftly negotiated sacred treaties.
- Nautiloids and Ammonites plumbed the deepest of philosophical depths.
- Thrinaxodons and Broomistegas cooperatively developed sophisticated aquacultural techniques.

These paleozoic folks learned well the values of peace, respect, cooperation and communication.

Then, of course, HUMANS came, big bullies who took whatever they wanted.

Violence is not the preferred way of those undersigned of QUEEN SUNSHINE BRIGHTSPINE'S ACCORDS, but something must be done, surely. For now, the HUMANS keep to their apple forest, but the tales of those displaced speak of naught but the wretched and rapacious nature of HUMANITY.

Very Pretty Paleozoic Pals: Permian Nations contains:

- 18 new Backgrounds of playable prehistoric critters.
- A terse-but-evocative overview of all notable cultures and locales in the *Wide River Valley* and its surroundings.
- Lots of Quick Charts to help you create new *Villages* and npcs on the fly as players explore this strange, cute land.
- Two Introductory Adventures: one suitable for characters generated using the Backgrounds presented herein as well as "normal" Troika! characters visiting this Sphere, the other written with characters native to Permian Nations in mind.
- Dozens of NPCs.
- Fantastic and Antagonistic Beasts ripped from the paleontological record.
- A positive glut of decadently whimsical illustrations.
- And finally: a terrible timeline of the possible conquering of the Valley by the pitiless ***Count Joehaund Lizardbane!***

Intro

Under the warm sun, kissed by shallow-ocean breezes, the folk of the *Wide River Valley* grew and prospered for generations. As more and more the borders of the different peoples met, tensions began to rise. Beneath a thick fog of impending violence, **Queen Sunshine Brightspine** of the **Xenacanthus** sharks organized the impossible.

A great meeting of all interested folk was held on *Gold Stone Island*, the heart of the *Brightspine Queendom*. Through her tireless efforts, understanding was reached, and the BRIGHTSPINE ACCORDS were writ into being.

These ACCORDS declared goodwill betwixt, peaceful right of passage through, and recognition of each member's territory, as well as each member-nation's self-sovereignty therein. The undersigned nations further added to the Accord a VIRTUE, central to their people, but to which all might aspire. **Dean Longshell** of the *Nautiloid and Ammonite Marine Conservancy* brought KNOWLEDGE at the behest of his peoples. **Queen Sunshine** of the *Xenacanthus Wide River Queendom* of course enshrined COOPERATION into the ACCORDS. The **Gathering of Mothers** from the *Dimetrodon Marshland Territories* most valued SELF EXPRESSION. The **Council of Elders** from the *Broomistega and Thrinaxodon Allied Protectorates*, as always, offered up FRIENDSHIP.

Each learned from the others. They traded goods and thoughts, intermingled freely through the years. For the most part, all was happy in the humid sunshine of the *Wide River Valley*.

However:

Around the time the ACCORDS were signed, an earthquake and its ensuing mudslides decimated a lonely County in a desolate Duchy on a distant world. The wreckage somehow rent open the veil between worlds and time. A barrel of apples and a whole shitload of fertile black soil careened into the *Wide River Valley*.

An apple forest grew in the midst of this world's Permian period. It expanded year by year, rapidly subsuming other biomes.

The Permian Folks adapted well enough. For the most part cosmopolitan communities, of all undersigned Species and many more, thrived in the alien forest. The forest itself kept expanding with the efficacy of floral futurity.

Then, the second son of a minor Duke of that distant Sphere stumbled through a disk of shadows and found a new world to exploit. The local 'beasts' objected to this exploitation in an unexpectedly direct and vocal way.

His iron-wrapped men slew the "obvious demons" with fusil, sword and vicious abandon. Even the river itself was spat full of wicked Spells and cruel curses by the fell and brutal HUMAN magi.

The surviving people fled in tears. Few HUMANS have ventured out of their apple forest since then, but everyone knows: one day they will.

For now, the ACCORDS and their fabulous peace are the Truth of the Land.

IMPORTANT QUESTION:

Q: What do you do, as, like, players in this happy-fairly-peaceful land?

A: Lots of things.

Most of the Backgrounds imply (or explicitly state) character motivations. The running theme here is "wandering." Characters explore for all sorts of reasons (Backgrounds pg 7). Along the way there are villages and nomadic families. These NPCs might pose direct problems ("Hello, I'm going to eat you.") or have problems of their own they could use help with ("Those *Secodontosaurus* meanies moved in and now we have to walk half a day just to get clean water!"). Players are encouraged to chase down whichever of these problems are most interesting to them. Players are also encouraged to run away from URANOCENTRODONS and INOSTRANCEVIA.

There's also the ongoing menace of HUMANITY, invasive species that we are. Defending this relatively peaceful and earnest land seems like something worth doing. Adventure #1 details the first incursion of the HUMANS into the Permian Nations.

There are also some deep mystical mysteries to be investigated in this warm, bucolic world. Adventure #2 skews in that direction.

ANOTHER IMPORTANT QUESTION, this one of MANNERS & MURDER:

What is and is not a thinking being, a person? You see, all the Undersigned nations are carnivores, so...

The Most Basic Rule of Civilized Consumption:

If an animal asks you not to eat them: please do not eat them.

All the animals below communicate and are not supposed to eat each other:

- *Xenacanths* and *Acanthode Sharks.*
- *Thrinaxodons* and some other therapsids, but not all.
- *Broomistegas* and some very few other amphibians, but not all.
- Both Whorled and Conical *Nautiloids.*
- *Giant Ammonites*, but no others.
- *Bivalves, Reptiles* and *Bugs* are almost always ok! (at least on this Sphere...)
- This list is not at all comprehensive.

So, for the most part, someone will tell you if they're not supposed to be eaten; it's a little embarrassing, but, hey, everyone makes mistakes.

It's also generally considered bad form to eat creatures similar to your present company (e.g. try not to eat other amphibians around *Broomistegas).*

Optional Rule for this Sphere: characters taken to 0 or less Stamina can be incapacitated, rather than outright slain, according to the intent of the victor. If there is no victor (e.g. falling down a hole): mourn them and all the terrible accidents of life.

Another *Optional Rule* for characters from this Sphere: most Backgrounds are from species notably smaller than those depicted in the Troika! rulebook (except *Ulemosaurs* and *Ammonites*). Thus:

- *Dimetrodons* and *Thrinaxodons* can carry up to 8 items before suffering the effects of encumbrance.
- *Broomistega, Xenacanthus* and *Nautiloids* can carry 6 items before becoming encumbered. Further, they cannot carry large items without dropping everything else and being encumbered.
- *Ammonites* can carry the usual 12 items before becoming encumbered.
- *Ulemosaurs* can carry 14 items before becoming encumbered.

Backgrounds

WHEN CREATING A NEW CHARACTER IN THE WIDE RIVER VALLEY ROLL 1D6 AND 1D3.		
1	*Dimetrodon*	
	1	Retired Matriarch
	2	Real Wild Child
	3	Fern Hag
2	*Thrinaxodon*	
	1	Inventor Errant
	2	Digger for Hire
	3	Lizard Keeper
3	*Broomistega*	
	1	Insatiably Curious Seeker
	2	Meditative Hunter
	3	Layabout
4	*Ulemosaurus*	
	1	Chronicler
	2	Clay Cartographer
	3	Trader
5	*Xenacanthus*	
	1	Keepers of Accord
	2	Oldstone Bringer
	3	Newly Becursed
6	*Marine*	
	1	Wizarding Nautiloid
	2	Natural Philosopher Nautiloid
	3	Giant Ammonite

Dimetrodon Backgrounds

4'-5' long, 90-130 pound quadrupeds with thick, hairless skin and spiny sails down their backs. Capable of using forelimbs as hands and arms, but only while awkwardly balancing on their tails. *Dimetrodons* mostly come in cool pastel colors, often offset with a pale magenta or sunset orange.

Dimetrodons take their appearance into their own claws. Self expression is the highest value, the very point of being for some synapsids. Polished stone accessories, claw-knit fabrics and especially flowers are hugely popular.

Flowering plants have only existed in the territories for 2 or 3 generations, so it's still the sort of thing very old *Dimetrodons* might complain about.

Dimetrodons live and love in open marshlands about the bends of the Wide River. For the most part, the vibrant folk reside with extended family. They've got little architecture beyond the careful stacking of stones to best catch and keep the warm rays of the rising sun. Most families also maintain a performing space for theater, dancing, fashion shows and the like. Performance is Art is Life Itself, after all.

All *Dimetrodons* do Unarmed Damage as Modest Beast.

1. Retired Matriarch

You have lived long, seen the tides of fashion crash and return. The burden of leadership has passed to your younger sisters, daughters, nieces. Your bones still yet hold true — in your mind still shines the CONSTELLATIONS OF WISDOM. Perhaps it is time to walk the wider world.

POSSESSIONS
- BLACK DIADEM OF AUTHORITY (symbol of wisdom in *Dimetrodon* culture).
- CROCK OF AMPHIBIANS IN BONELESS FISH ASPIC (3 Provisions).
- BRIGHT, POLISHED STONE.
- VIBRANT SAIL SHAWL.

ADVANCED SKILLS
2 Constellation of Seeing (pg 26)
2 Etiquette
1 Biting
1 Dancing
1 Singing
1 Tracking

2. Real Wild Child

It didn't take you long to understand: you've wandered into dangerous places against your family's wishes since you were a hatchling. Warnings are advertisements of adventure! You're your own synapsid and you've got the chops to make your own damn way in the wider world.

POSSESSIONS
- 7 POUCHES OF MUD PIGMENTS.
- HOLLOW REED and 1D6 THIN, POISONED DARTS (Damage as Unarmed, Test Luck or become Unconscious for 1d6 minutes).
- 20' OF STRONG BRAIDED ROPE.
- 9 DRIED AMPHIBIAN PROVISIONS.
- WATERSKIN.

ADVANCED SKILLS
3 Tracking
2 Biting
2 Blowgun Pffting
2 Trapping
1 Fishing
-1 General Lore

3. Fern Hag

It is terrible to think, but sometimes an egg gets lost, though no babe is left to cry alone. Ancestor spirits heard you and took you in. Ghosts of dead relatives raised you up and kept you safe, but now they rest. Still you know their love and wisdom. Still you speak with them in dreams.

POSSESSIONS
- NECKLACE OF 13 ANCESTOR TEETH.
- COLLECTION OF DRIED MEDICINAL FERNS (+1 to Healing, 7 uses).
- MANTLE OF LIVING BLOOMS.
- 7 UNLUCKY KNUCKLEBONES OF A DROWNED SYNAPSID, discovered under a full moon.
- DISCONCERTING WHITE EYES.
- THE LOVE OF HALF-SLEEPING GHOSTS.

ADVANCED SKILLS
3 Constellation of Dead Wisdom (pg 24)
2 Dimetrodon Territories Fern Herbology (pg 24)
1 Spell — Call the Voidstar Constellation (pg 26)
1 Spell — Banish Spirits
1 Spell — Helping Hands
1 Biting
1 Fishing
1 Healing

SPECIAL
Rather than suffering Stamina loss from casting a Spell, you may throw aside 1 Unlucky Knucklebone with an apology.

Thrinaxodon Backgrounds

2-3' long, 70-90 pound sociable, burrowing quadrupeds with sharp digging claws and pale green fur, glowing softly in the dark. Their burrows are elaborate, highly decorated and often shared with other creatures, especially *Broomistega* Amphibians. Companionship is central to most *Thrinaxodon* cultures, extending readily to other species.

Thrinaxodons often practice aquaculture, keeping Schools of BONELESS FISH in flooded chthonic chambers. Some keep HERDS OF LIZARDS amongst the expanding grasslands in their territories. Still others hunt insects, catch fish and aestivate during dry spells, in harmony with the old ways.

These lil' therapsids live in seasonally dry prairie lands to the west of the *Wide River*, a landscape quickly being dominated by various grasses, as native seed ferns and clubmosses simply cannot compete.

Thrinaxodons can stand upright on their hind legs, and their cute little hands are quite deft. Due to sharing a border with *County Lizardbane*, almost every *Thrinaxodon* has seen a HUMAN BEING or knows someone who has!

1. Inventor Errant

Fresh club moss branches have a much lower sproing-factor than the apple twigs you've managed to gather, even when the twigs are quite dry. Not everyone knows this — maybe just you? You investigate and dream. The physical world can be your friend if you just learn how to talk to her. With a lever, a fulcrum, a little clever and a counterweight you can change lives... or at the very least have an interesting ride!

POSSESSIONS
- LIZARD SKIN BACKPACK.
- LARGE BALL OF FLAXEN STRING.
- 20' TWISTED ROPE.
- BUNDLE OF CONSTRUCTION/JOURNAL STICKS.
- WOODEN HAMMER.
- COPPER KNIFE or STONE DRILL.
- BOW-TYPE FIRE STARTER (+1 to Fire Building).
- HUNK OF COPPER ORE.
- STONE CRUCIBLE.

ADVANCED SKILLS
2 Fire Building
2 Idiosyncratic Mathmology
2 Inventing (pg 24)
1 Burrow Construction
1 Copper Smelting
1 Sculpting Casts for Smelting
0 Esoteric Knowledge (pg 24)

2. Digger for Hire

Sometimes a burrow, even a whole hillside, gets too crowded and you just gotta see what's on the other side of the bend. You've left your family and friends behind, bringing your Skills to where they might be needed. Maybe you'll start your own burrow one day or find a new home among distant lands. The world is wide for walking; some folks see this for the true blessing it is.

POSSESSIONS
- *ROUGH LINEN DUFFEL BAG*.
- *STONE FELLING AXE* (as Axe, breaks on Fumble).
- *FISHING POLE, LINE, 1D6 WOODEN HOOKS*.
- *STONE SICKLE* (as Knife, breaks on Fumble) and *WOODEN HAMMER*.
- *CLAY JAR OF FISH PASTE* (7 Provisions).
- *PAIR OF FRIENDSHIP STONES* (pg 25) or *+1 LUCK* and a **HEAVY HEART**.

ADVANCED SKILLS
3 Digging (pg 24)
2 Burrow Construction
2 Climb
1 Fishing
1 Trailblazing
1 Tracking
1 Strength

3. Lizard Keeper

In the long grasses you tame the wild lizards and make them your herd. You lead them to water, protect them, bring them to shelter in a storm. You also eat them and craft their skin into clothing. It's a weird relationship. Life has been a bit cruel lately — maybe it's time to wander somewhere new?

POSSESSIONS
- *LONG LIZARD HERDING STICK* (as Club).
- *LIZARD-LEATHER OUTFIT* (as Light Armour).
- *HERD OF 3D6 EATING LIZARDS* and *1D3 RIDING-SIZED LIZARDS*.
- *12 DRIED LIZARD PROVISIONS* and *2 LARGE WATERSKINS*.
- *MUSSEL SHELL CASTANETS*.
- *2 LARGE WATERSKINS*.
- *STONE KNIFE* (as Knife, breaks on Fumble).
- *PAIR OF FRIENDSHIP STONES* (pg 25) or *+1 LUCK* and a **HEAVY HEART**.

ADVANCED SKILLS
4 Lizard Herding
2 Primitive Tanning
2 Stick Fighting
1 Butchering
1 Lizard Riding
1 Tracking

Broomistega Backgrounds

1½-2' long, 25-35 pound brightly colored amphibians with long, broad snouts, cosmopolitan distribution and even more cosmopolitan attitudes. These little ones are everywhere: everywhere there's fresh water and somewhere to hide from bigger, meaner things.

They've developed mutually beneficial relationships with all manner of unexpected species, most famously with the *Thrinaxodons*. The combination of *Broomistegas'* aquatic expertise and *Thrinaxodons'* burrowing Skills is what has made their aquacultural success so spectacular.

"It's important to be good at what you do. Though, no matter your skill, there's nothing that's not better with a helping claw."—COMMON BROOMISTEGA APHORISM.

Like *Dimetrodons*, *Broomistega's* can stand up while balancing on their tails.

1. Insatiably Curious Seeker

What digs a burrow like that? What's over there? Is that positively giant therapsid over yonder a nice fellow? It's best to just go find out, you reckon.

There's no danger of missed opportunities if you take them all! At the very least you oughtta ask each opportunity a few questions, right?

Not everyone's as friendly as you, and not everywhere is as safe as home: you know this, now. Hey, you're still kicking, though, and you've learned so much so far.

POSSESSIONS
- LIZARD-LEATHER BELT FESTOONED WITH VARIOUS POUCHES.
- 10' ROPE.
- Several INTERESTING ROCKS.
- TINY SLING (Damage as Unarmed).
- 6 LESS INTERESTING ROCKS for the SLING.
- 5 SMALL JARS OF FISH PASTE Provisions.
- WANDERLUST.

ADVANCED SKILLS
4 Dodge
3 Slinging Stones
2 Swimming
1 Climbing
1 General Knowledge
1 Etiquette
-2 Strength

2. Meditative Hunter

Slow, steady movements, cautious, deliberate — patience is everything. In the vegetative muck below the muddy waters you move travel, inches by the hour. The sharp eyes on top of your broad skull defocus in the hunter's meditation as the words of your forebearers percolate in indistinct sensation.

Then: something swims overhead. Before you comprehend why, you wait. The clicking becomes a conscious sensation: the beating wings of a giant dragonfly. It carries off the biggest fish in the School. You wait. The clicking dies away in the distance. You're still spoilt for choice when it's time to strike.

POSSESSIONS
- *HEAVILY OILED, WATER RESISTANT BAG.*
- *SACRED LUMP OF SALT* (+1 Luck unless you lose it).
- *COPPER SPEAR* (Damage as Dagger).
- 8 *DRIED FISH PROVISIONS*

ADVANCED SKILLS
4 Stealth
3 Tracking
3 Spear Fighting
2 Swimming
1 Climbing
-2 Strength

3. Layabout

Let's be honest: the best thing about friends and family is that you ain't got to do so much. Yeah, you probably care about 'em, but that ain't nothing compared to a good nap or a nibble of fish you didn't have to hunt up. Of course, folks only put up with that for so long. You're pretty damn charming, so that helps... but only so much. Still, there's always more ~~rubes~~ friends to be had around the bend.

POSSESSIONS
- *ILL-FITTING BACKPACK.*
- *SOMEONE ELSE'S HAMMOCK.*
- 3d6 *PRETTY, POLISHED STONES*, Stolen.
- *PURLOINED FISHING POLE.*

ADVANCED SKILLS
3 Roguish Charm
3 Etiquette
2 Sleight of Hand
1 Swimming
1 Fishing
1 Stealth
1 Dodge
-3 Strength

Ulemosaurus Backgrounds

7'–9' long, 350–450 pound cumbersome, herbivorous, quadrupedal synapsids who don't maintain territories. Rather, they lumber about, looking for tasty conifers to eat and new experiences to pursue. Their steady diet of piney shrubs gifts their blue-green skin with a deeply resinous scent.

Whenever two *Ulemosaurs* meet in their wanderings they exchange stories to see if they might be compatible mates. The ritual is the same regardless of gender or the seriousness of either party. Family units tend to homestead wherever the parents met, just long enough to take their children into adulthood. Though it isn't exactly rare to see an *Ulemosaur* settled into village life, their reputation as wanderers is well earned.

Despite having no governmental bodies to sign the ACCORDS, most *Ulemosaurs* wholeheartedly agree with their sentiments. As gregarious herbivores, they have long been welcome except in the most xenophobic of communities.

Ulemosaurs cannot stand at all, and rely on well-trained pets to act as their surrogate hands. All have 4–5" thick skulls, which combined with their huge size and great strength gives their headbutt the Damage of a MAUL. Their dense build and heavy bones also grant them the equivalent of MODEST ARMOUR.

1. Chronicler

Words are inconstant until you set them down in wood, clay or stone. The world around feels much the same way: write to remember, write to reveal, write to understand. Existence is this tangled strings of stories, unraveling into oblivion. You write it all down, for yourself and for those who come after you.

POSSESSIONS
- 1d3 GIANT DRAGONFLIES (raven-sized, fast and distractible Hirelings).
- WOVEN SEED FERN SADDLEBAGS.
- CLAW SHARPENING STONE.
- 7 SCRIBING LOGS, Blank.
- 8 SCRIBING LOGS, Full of Observations, Tales and Musings.
- POUCH FULL OF GRUBS (Dragonfly Treats).
- DOZENS OF LOOSE STICKS (for quick notes and/or snacks).

ADVANCED SKILLS
3 Strength
2 General Knowledge
1 Current Affairs
1 Dragonfly Training
1 History
1 Natural History
1 Take Notes

2. Clay Cartographer

The world just makes more sense after you've sculpted a map. When you feel the shape of the land underneath your claws, you can truly *understand*. The practical nature of maps doesn't escape you — it's wonderful your creations can help others find their way, but there's just nothing like the naked joy of sculpting a map of somewhere new, even if no one else ever touches it.

POSSESSIONS
- 1 SLOW-MOVING EUNOTOSAURUS (pg 82, as loyal Hireling).
- CLAW-KNIT SADDLEBAG.
- POUCH OF FINE CLAY.
- 2d6 CLAY MAPS.
- 1 COLORFUL POLISHED STONE.

ADVANCED SKILLS
4 Sculptural Cartography
3 Geography
3 Strength
2 Eunotosaurus Training

3. Trader

Trading is much more than exchanging goods — a merchant is welcome wherever they wander. They bring not only goods but news. You are the connection between distant points. A treatise on tensile strength carved into stones by Nautiloid and Ammonite students makes its way to the **Thrinaxodon** engineer who will do so much with it, only because of you.

POSSESSIONS
- 1d6 DRAGONFLY ASSISTANTS (pg 25).
- CUTE LITTLE HAT.
- VERY NICE SADDLEBAGS.
- 1d6+1 BUNDLES OF TRADE-GOODS of your choice.
- POUCH FULL OF GRUBS (Dragonfly Treats).
- 12+1d6 BEAUTIFUL ROCKS.
- JAR OF PINEY RESIN (YUM!).
- 40' BRAIDED ROPE.

ADVANCED SKILLS
4 Barter
2 Dragonfly Training
2 Etiquette
1 Geography
1 Headbutt Fighting

Xenacanthus Backgrounds

3-4' long, 20-45 pound freshwater sharks sporting a poisonous spine projecting backwards from their heads. Their eel-like bodies are rich azure to pale seafoam green, bespeckled or overtaken by sunset hues.

Xenacanthus live in Schools of extended families swearing cooperation with the ACCORDS. Below the waterline, alliances and friendships flourish. *Xenacanthus* and *Eurypterid* folks work to ensure the supply of DELICIOUS SHELLFISH AND AQUATIC SNAILS along the *Wide River* and her many tributaries.

Though nomadic Schools of fish in a healthy ecosystem have little need for possessions, those swimming the world above learned the value of keeping a few useful things on their persons. In many ways, Dance and Storytelling function similarly to prized possessions in other cultures. The average *Xenacanthus* would be unconcerned if you ate the last snail she'd been saving for an after-nap snack — no one owns the river's bounty. However, if you copied her dance moves, she would be U P S E T.

The venom gland of adult *Xenacanths* produces 1d6 stab-doses/day; up to ten stab-doses can be stored.

DAMAGE ROLL➡	1	2	3	4	5	6	7+
Maddeningly Painful Venom	2	3	4	5	6	13	18

Otherwise the spine does 1 Damage.

Finally, their sturdy, twin-pointed teeth are great at crunching through heavy shells and even soft rocks.

1. Keepers of Accord

There are many flavors of surprising asceticism amongst the smiling *Xenacanthus* Sharks. Cooperation is often negotiation; concession and compromise are expected. Those willing to concede their whole lives to the cause of euphonious ACCORD are known as Keepers. Through sacred fasts, strange rituals and perseverant conviction, Keepers gain entry to the Air. There you and your brethren swim, that the land may be kept in accord with the water.

You swim into *Secodontosaur* shallow swamps, *Thrinaxodon* burrows and *Dimetrodon* amphitheaters to keep the LIGHT OF HARMONIOUS ACCORD shining.

POSSESSIONS
- COURIER BASKET.
- 3 BAGS OF MUD CLAMS (3 Provisions).
- 33' HIGH QUALITY BRAIDED ROPE.
- LANCE-LIKE-A-GLINT-ON-WATER (pg 25).

ADVANCED SKILLS
2 Lance-like-a-glint-on-water
2 Spell — Control Rope (pg 26)
2 Navigation
2 Etiquette
1 Spell — Light
1 Spine Stab

2. Oldstone Bringer

There are stones your mother should have warned you about — I bet she did. On such stones powerful seals, summons and sigils lie waiting to be tried, etched by generations of magnetotactic bacteria aligning to the twists in this Sphere's magnetic field. Such perturbations may be footprints left by exoreality entities from long before the planet's crust cooled. Don't get the wrong idea, though — these symbols aren't evil, not at all. They are dangerous, though. Your mother probably worries.

POSSESSIONS

- 3 SWALLOWED STONES (each etched with a Luck rune, +1 total Luck).
- DANGLING SPINE CHARM (denotes status as an Oldstone Binder).

ADVANCED SKILLS

2 Spell — Optimal Oxygen Delivery & Locomotion Rune (pg 27)
1 Spell — Roll on chart below*
1 Spell — Roll on chart below*
1 Spell — Roll on chart below*
1 Spell — Random Troika! Spell
1 Spell — Random Troika! Spell
1 Spell — Implementation of an Unlikely Presence (Summoning)
-1 Strength

SPECIAL

Oldstone Bringers cast Spells by signing sigils through the movement of their bodies — swim-casting, you might call it. They need speak nothing, but require room to twist themselves through the paths of unreal symbols.

SPELLS	
1	Dual Probability Cycle Grapheme (pg 27)
2	Scale Reassessment Upward Glyph (pg 27)
3	Scale Reassessment Downward Glyph (pg 27)
4	Anthropomorphizing Interpreter Sigil (pg 26)
5	Extreme Carbon Molecule Excitation Microburst Diagrams (pg 27)
6	Hyper-efficient Photosynthetic Epidermal Transmogrification Pictogram (pg 27)

†Rerolls indicate higher Skill in that particular Spell.

*Rerolls indicate higher Skill in that particular Spell.

3. Newly Becursed
You didn't deserve this.

2 dozen years ago, when the HUMAN magi spit their cruel curses into the tributary streams of their territory, a new river was born of *Xenacanthus* tears. Hundreds were forced from their homes, forced from the waters themselves and into the sky! Many of those unfortunate folk have already left this Sphere in search of a cure or a new home.

Even still, the curse continues. Distant relatives of those initially affected sometimes spontaneously develop the curse as well.

The river has been stolen from you; now you swim through the air.

POSSESSIONS
- SMALL MUD-FILLED POUCH WITH A FEW AQUATIC SNAILS (1 Provision, a delicacy).
- A SAD SONG IN YOUR HEART.

ADVANCED SKILLS
2 Crunch
2 Swim-Dancing
1 Clam/Mussel Digging
1 Spine Stab
0 Tracking
-1 Strength

SPECIAL
You can swim through the air, which is a lot like flying, but lil' magic sparkles pop out of your tail when you move. That's conspicuous, especially in the dark. Going higher than 15' is uncomfortable. Also, you can't manipulate objects with much precision b/c fins not thumbs.

Marine Backgrounds

Nautiloids

Shelled marine molluscs around the size of a large HUMAN head. Some have conical shells while others possess the more familiar whorly type shells. They're often colored in oceanic blues with dayglow pink, orange and yellow. From the bottom half of their faces sprout dozens of delicate tentacles. They dwell in a long shallow bay into which the Wide River drains.

Nautiloids gather into literal Schools, in great underwater Academic Arenas. There they learn (and debate at l e n g t h) magic, mathmology, natural history and more.

Through intense sorceries and an unparalleled reservoir of raw will, **Dean Longshell** built the mostly empty city of *Terragyre* with a single Spell. The city currently hosts 34 wizarding acolytes from other worlds, 13 full time educators, golden barge dry-docks and dozens of semi-permanent/ transient residents.

The world of the *Nautiloids* only grows less provincial through time.

Nautiloid Shells grant them LIGHT ARMOUR.

Giant Ammonites

Spiral-shelled marine/terrestrial molluscs, 5-7' tall with 5 broad, muscular and multi-colored tentacles. Each section of their dense, multicolored shells is marked by heavy ridges.

There is no *Ammonite* culture. Each awakens alone and fully-grown somewhere off the continental shelf, troubled by dreams of fire and iron, as well as a compulsion to make their way shoreward. Along the way, *Ammonites* almost inevitably run across a *Nautiloid School*. In *Nautiloid Schools*, by long tradition, *Giant Ammonites* are awarded as much education as they wish. Eventually the drive toward land overwhelms curiosity...

Shell as MODEST ARMOUR. Thick leathery tentacles do Damage as CLUB.

1. Wizarding Nautiloid

When one can study methods with which to manipulate the very foundations of reality, why would one study anything else? The dense, cryptic and rambling prose of sorcerous souls might have been a deterrent to some, but not you. You absorbed every mystical lecture and thaumaturgical demonstration you could attend. You learned the laborious arts of levitation and breathing. Your classmates may have found academic recognition, but you hold the levers that move worlds.

POSSESSIONS
- *THAUMATURGICAL ROD* (pg 25).
- *WIZARD POCKETS* (pg 25).
- *3 SMALL SWARMS OF TRIOPS* (Each Swarm is 1 Provision).
- *2 SMALL SWARMS OF TRILOBITES* (Each Swarm is 1 Provision).

ADVANCED SKILLS
3 Spell — Lungs (pg 27)
2 Telekinesis
1 Spell — Random Spell
1 Spell — Random Spell
1 Spell — Random Spell
0 Levitate (see Special)

SPECIAL
Levitate is something most Nautiloids can do as they need or wish to. It should only be checked when attempting to dodge or outrun someone.

2. Natural Philosopher Nautiloid

There is so, so much of the natural world you've yet to see. Sure, you've learned a great deal in School, and you've got pet theories for almost everything. Still though, maybe it's time to put it to the test? Maybe you can do some good out in the wider world? Regardless, you'll get much better data if you actually collect some data.

POSSESSIONS
- 6 THIN STONE TABLETS, half-full of Theories and Musings.
- STONE SCRATCH AWL.
- 3 BUNDLES OF FISH JERKY.

ADVANCED SKILLS
3 Natural History
2 Theorizing
1 Mathmology
1 Telekinesis
1 Spell — Lungs (pg 27)
1 Levitate

3. Giant Ammonite

You have made it to the shore, and the terrible pressure you felt is gone. You breathe through unexpected lungs. You've learned much from your very distant Nautiloid kin. Capricious dreams and unfamiliar memories have taught you many things as well. There is still so much to understand. Something woke you from the deeps, from a life you can't remember. Now you wander on unfamiliar shores.

POSSESSIONS
- *MANY QUESTIONS.*

ADVANCED SKILLS
2 Strength
1 Fighting with Weapon of Choice
1 Natural History
1 Etiquette
1 Iron Smelting
1 Blacksmithing
1 Fire Building
1 Tracking
1 Trapping

Advanced Skills

Constellation of Dead Wisdom

Successful use allows a **Fern Hag** to commune with their ancestors while sleeping and learn what the ancestors know:

FAMILY HISTORY.

DIMETRODON MYTHS AND LEGENDS.

THE NATURE OF SPIRITS AND GHOSTS.

The ancestors can also see, smell, taste, feel and hear anywhere a **Dimetrodon** could get to, within 1 mile of the dreaming **Fern Hag**. May only be taught to the living by the dead.

Constellation of Seeing

Allows the **Dimetrodon Matriarch** to determine the truth of one statement spoken in her presence, at the cost of 1d6 Luck. Requires 10 minutes of unbroken concentration. The speaker feels the intense scrutiny of the stars, liars and false-talkers glowing faintly.

Digging

Can dig out 3 cubic feet of loose soil in 1 one minute, (1d6+1 minutes in stony or otherwise difficult soil). On failure it takes twice as long. Can only be learned by burrowing critters.

Dimetrodon Territories Fern Herbology

Can be used to gather a collection of MEDICINAL FERNS. Requires 1d6 hours and being in *Dimetrodon Territories*.

Esoteric Knowledge

Can be tested to know or intuit 1 fact about any given situation.

Inventing

Player describes, in at least a vague way, how the invention is to be constructed and its operation. Success means it functions as intended, failure indicates embarrassing collapse. Double sixes indicate failure in a dangerous and spectacular way. The degree of danger involved should be pretty easy to suss out, and ought to be discussed explicitly. Exact explanations with little risk of failure should be allowed to work.

Example: build a seesaw to distract the **Ammonite** children so the elders can perform a ritual uninterrupted. There's no real risk of harm beyond a bruised tentacle or chipped shell. It's easy to see how you yourself might go get it done in the backyard. However, if you're trying to lash together a trebuchet to defend a **Xenacanthus** School from HUMAN fisherfolk, the dice need to come out. Failure means someone could get very hurt, possibly killed.

Items

Pair of Friendship Stones

When given to a true friend, one stone always knows which direction the other stone lies. The *Thrinaxodon* or friend simply asks their stone "Which way to [name]?"; the stone rises with a friendly gleam, and slowly floats a few inches toward the companion stone. Keeping pace with its owner, the stone leads the way to the missing friend. Upon being gifted (this can ONLY happen once), both the Giver and Receiver gain permanent +1 Luck. Both stones disintegrate upon the death of either friend. These stones are a magical gift given to almost every *Thrinaxodon* on the day of their birth.

Lance-like-a-glint-on-water

A thin, 2' long forever-frozen reflection of sunshine glinting off the river. It breaks the surface alongside each *Keeper* as they take their sacred vows and swim into the air. Each Lance remains within 12' of its shark, under their total mental control. Damage as Spear, weighs nothing, cannot be broken so long as its *Keeper* breaks no oath.

Thaumaturgical Rod

Reduces the Stamina cost to cast Spells by 1. Stamina permanently reduced by one if lost or broken.

Wizard Pockets

Invisible pocket dimensions hanging off of you like magical cargo shorts.

Giant Dragonfly Assistants

The size of a large raven. Treat as quick and distractible Hirelings.

Spells

Anthropomorphizing Interpreter Sigil (3)

A cutesy, little anthropomorphized hologram of the caster happily explains aloud all communication happening in the caster's presence which the caster would not have otherwise understood. Everyone can see them. They are LOUD and CHEERFUL. Lasts 24 hours or until dismissed.

Call the Voidstar Constellation (4)

Causes an orb of perfect, permanent darkness the size of a big melon to come into existence in the caster's palm. It can be physically moved about by the caster as though it were a physical object, something like an inflated balloon. The caster is able to anchor the darkness orb to objects like a wall, a sword or even someone's face. Otherwise the orb just remains in whatever position it was in when the caster let it go. Those who think to try can Test Luck to manipulate the orb.

A caster can have no more than 7 of these orbs in existence. Creating the 8th orb destroys the 1st. If more than 6 orbs are within 40' of one another there is a 1-in-6 chance they spell out a voidstar sigil and all life in 1d6×10' must Test Luck or Die. Assume flora and very small life forms automatically fail this Test. If more than 13 orbs are within 40' of one another THE SIGIL IS INEVITABLE.

Constellation Ferocior (1d6 years of life)

Sphenecadon Star Witches sacrifice 1d6 years of their life to cast Spells. Successful casting transforms the Sphenecadon into a Ferocior state for 3 days or until the Spell is ended. Their stats are replaced with the following: [SKLL:**10** STAM:**18** INIT:**3** ARMR:**0** LARGE BEAST] and they gain the following Special: regenerate 1 Stamina each time an initiative token is pulled.

Constellation of Vitality (1d6 years of life)

Sphenecadon Star Witches sacrifice 1d6 years of their life to cast Spells. Tied somehow to the hormonal magic of adrenaline, this Spell allows its subject to regenerate 1 Stamina per combat round but only during life or death combat. This Spell begins and ends with fight-or-flight chemistry.

Control Rope (1-3)

Caster can manipulate a 33' length of rope as a direct extension of their will. The rope's strength and general efficacy are equal to the Stamina paid to cast. Lasts 1d6 hours or until dismissed. However, this Spell only controls ropes 33' long; cutting the line immediately dispels all magic from the fibers.

Dual Probability Cycle Grapheme (1-10)

Causes an exact duplicate of the caster to form several feet to their left, for a number of minutes equal to the Stamina paid. The duplicate and original can then act separately as the player wishes, so long as they work on no tasks directly together (e.g. they can't attack the same enemy or try to force open the same door). There aren't actually two of the caster, just two possibilities occurring simultaneously. At the end of the duration the player must decide which probability to continue with as the other rapidly fades away.

Extreme Carbon Molecule Excitation Microburst Diagrams (5)

Can only be cast on carbon based lifeforms. The center-mass of the victim glows softly in blue-green light for a heartbeat, before random chemical bonds impossibly sunder on the creature's exterior, replacing skin, shell and bark with the black dust of elemental carbon and the smell of ozone.

Damage Roll➡	1	2	3	4	5	6	7+
Microbursts	3	6	9	12	13	13	17

Hyper-Efficient Photosynthetic Epidermal Transmogrification Pictogram (2)

Subject's dermis turns spring-growth green for 1d6-1 days (if zero days the Spell lasts for 1d6 hours). In this state, 1 hour of relative stillness in the sunshine is the equivalent of 1 Provision.

Lungs (2)

Caster grows a pair of functioning lungs at the expense of their gills. Lasts until dismissed. Stamina cost cannot be healed so long as Spell is in effect.

Optimal Oxygen Delivery & Locomotion Rune (1d6)

Allows the caster to swim through the air as though it were as dense as water, while also extracting sufficient oxygen from the air impossibly through their gills. Stamina cost cannot be healed until dismissed.

Scale Reassessment Upward Glyph (3)

Subject doubles in volume and mass for 1d6 minutes. Can only be cast on creatures or objects fitting (before growth) within a 10'x10' cube.

Scale Reassessment Downward Glyph (3)

Subject gets halved in volume and mass for 1d6 minutes. Can only be cast on creatures or objects fitting (before growth) within a 10'x10' cube.

Nautiloid and Ammonite Marine Conservancy

The long shallow sea is another world, one those from the land cannot quite begin to understand: effortless motion, gravity degraded by buoyancy into near meaninglessness. The rhythmic jets of water from a hyponome or an undulating fin scoot you thoughtlessly along a day-glo landscape of life and color. Magenta coral and lavender cartilaginous fish, orange-red bivalves and shining spiny sharks, a magnificent ecosystem protected by long tradition and reasonable mutual interest.

Communities are distant and centered around *Academic Arenas*, each carefully carved from exposed stone near enough to sustainable food reserves. Given the relative rarity of both elements, the founding of a new community is a cause for incredible celebration.

Cooperation with other beings was of course necessary for the emergence of the Conservancy. Though they do not generally leave the marine environment, Conservancy participants such as the **Accanthode** spine-finned sharks, **Bembexia** sea snail and **Janassa** fish adhere to the spirit and letter of **Queen Brightspine's** Accords.

Terragyre

The *Marine Conservancy's* only terrestrial settlement. Atop an impossibly huge fossilized ammonite, 3,000' across, dozens of loaf-shaped, sandstone structures were conjured into being. The largest of them intersect to form the relatively new *Terrestrial-Marine Nautiloid Wizardry College*.

The College, much like the entirety of *Terragyre*, is the pet project of **Dean Longshell**. It is an experiment in not just deepening the *Conservancy's* ties to the surface nations, but also to the wider multiverse as well. *Terragyre* currently boasts not only the School but also the only Tavern and golden barge port on the planet. Not much more than that, though: 95% of the town is currently unoccupied.

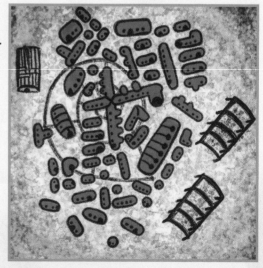

Xenacanthus Wide River Queendom

Under the eddies and currents cooperation thrives. Boundaries do not exist, save the edge of the water. Everyone's home is the entirety of the river.

Eurypterids turn the sandy river bottoms with their raking limbs, eating tiny gastropods and bringing up the larger brachiopods and bivalves for *Xenacanths* to smilingly munch. In turn, the *Xenacanthus* Schools provide protection by venomous spine and bright magics. Large predators are not allowed within the waters unless they swear to uphold the ACCORDS (excepting URANOCENTRADONS, who cannot safely be asked anything and must instead be avoided, at best).

Though the whole of the region up to the Redsand River is claimed as part of the Queendom, towards the northeastern edge of the *Dimetrodon* territories things begin to get fairly lawless. Predation by the likes of ANTEOSAURS and other larger critters becomes increasingly common the further upstream you go.

Gold Stone Island

On a rocky island in the heart of the *Wide River Queendom*, near to the western-most shore, QUEEN BRIGHTSPINE'S ACCORDS are displayed exactly as they were signed. The island is named after a huge erratic boulder surfaced in iron pyrite (fool's gold). Vegetation is sparse and little else can be found.

Keepers of the Accord finish training here, building small, temporary camps. More experienced Keepers teach the newer sharks various mores and manners of the surface world. These classes are infrequent (1-in-6 chance 2d6 Keepers are present). Otherwise, this island is a lonely monument...

Unless you go beneath the waves, in which case the frequent presence of **Queen Brightspine's court** keeps the surrounding waters a very busy place.

Silthome

Just over a sandy ridge on the southwest beach of *Silthead Island*, a group of Becursed *Xenacanthus* refugees founded a community 20 years ago. Since then it has become a haven for the iconoclastic and discontented. Dour *Dimetrodons*, angry *Xenacanths*, socially anxious *Broomistegas* and icily grim *Thrinaxodons* are just the beginning. Those who never felt at home elsewhere often wind up carried down the river and deposited here.

Thrinaxodon & Broomistega
Allied Protectorates

There was a time before friendship. There was a time when **Thrinaxodon** and **Broomistega** were predator and prey.

It was the hot, dry season that brought them together. **Soft Glow the Thrinaxodon** aestivated in his burrow, waiting out the terrible heat. The pond of **Patience Starlight the Broomistega** first shrank to a puddle, then to a crusting patch of mud beneath the relentless sun. In desperation, **Patience** fled into the nearest cool, dark place — **Softie's** burrow. She found a damp patch of soil, too near the snoring, glowing burrower within, but her skin ached for moisture. There she waited for 3 days, unsure of what to do.

Then, thunder peeled in the distance, and a subtle but intensifying vibration carried fear up through the pads of **Patience's** feet. FLASH FLOOD! She could not, she would not leave her unwitting host to drown. **Patience** poked and prodded, but still he would not awaken! She smacked his ribs, and **Soft Glow** barely stirred. In desperation, **Patience** bit his tail. It worked! He bounded out of the burrow, with her still clamped on, and just in time. As they spoke with one another atop a hillock turned island, a friendship was born.

They carried the message of interspecies cooperation and cohabitation far and wide. Since then many communities integrated and thrived. Aquaculture developed, and along with it the growth of interconnected burrows into towns and even cities.

Grasses are taking over the native fauna. Seed fern trees cannot take hold through the dense tangle of alien roots, and so grass and rolling hills, studded with coniferous bushes and aging scale-trees, have become the local landscape. In increasingly thin margins, tight against the waterways, native plants endure.

Towards the north end of the Protectorates, several **Ammonite** communities have been established on or near the beach.

Shadepool Burrows

Shadepool claims to be the very first community founded by *Soft Glow* and *Patience Starlight* (as do a number of other communities.) Shadepool is by far the largest city in not just the Protectorates but amongst them as a whole, with a population of nearly 7,000 souls. There are a few dozen structures built on the surface, but most of the city winds underground. Aquacultural ponds occupy the entire southern half of the tunnel complex. A huge *Berm* sits on the northeastern edge of the city, constructed from vast amounts of excavated earth, and continues to be built as more and more city is dug out from the ground.

Currently, *Mayor Budding Stillness* is actively recruiting other species to move to Shadepool. Nearly two dozen *Ulemosaur* households, an *Estemmenosuchus* family and even a smattering of *Sphenecadons* have answered their call.

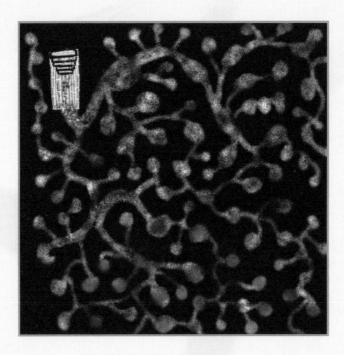

Dimetrodon Marshland Territories

This area exhibits lush green vegetation in all directions, broken only by sunning stones, shallow amphitheaters and the river's winding edge. For the most part flora here is still yet ferns, moss and the occasional squat cycad or ginkgo bush. Still though, some flowering grasses and low, ground-clinging vines have begun to overrun the native plants.

The presence of **Sphenecadons** amongst the occasional copse of scale or ginkgo trees, **Secodontosaurs** in many of the streams and **Edaphosaurs** anywhere there might be plants to munch certainly makes this seem like the land of sail-backed synapsids.

Very few integrated communities exist, despite broadly similar cultures and origin myths.

Starlight Xephyr Amphitheater

It was found, not built, or so the legend goes. A gift from capricious stars? Something more like a demand to be entertained; questions like that show how little one knows of the indifferent stars.

Most **Dimetrodons** don't seem to mind much — **Dimetrodon** culture is all about expressive performance. The end of the dry season marks the beginning of the celestial calendar year: for 9 days, all the stars are watching.

(This also marks the beginning of mating season.)

Every year, nearly every **Dimetrodon** who is able makes the trek to the amphitheater: a series of perfect, concentric circles cut into basalt bedrock like an inverted ziggurat. There the greatest artists in fashion, theater and song perform and compete with one another, for the stars must be kept at amused indifference, lest they turn to baleful disregard.

It's kind of a bonus that these sacred competitions are REALLY FUN TO WATCH.

Dry Wind Gap

A small, semi-permanent encampment sits between two lovely, dusty, orange-green hills. Right at the boundary between the arid uplands and the soft wet lowlands, strange travelers meet to exchange stories and goods betwixt the mostly-unconnected biomes and peoples.

County Lizardbane (Human Territory)

Apple and pine trees blanket a landscape of rolling rocky ridges, dotted by infrequent sugarloaf shaped peaks. Most intelligent life fled the region due to incessant and cruel HUMAN violence. Those still about speak as little as possible. Should one syllable land within a HUMAN's weird, mussel-shaped ears, the critter who spoke may be relentlessly hunted and slain.

Stumpgarden

Serfdom of vegetable farmers east of *Fort Deadfin*. Comprised of 30 family cabins, each with their own small gardens, scattered across 3 forested ridges.

Deadfin Village

10 buildings sit on either side of a short cobbled street, connected to *Fort Deadfin* across the *New River* by way of a crude wooden bridge. Each is the home and workshop of an artisan, busily building what-so-ever **The Count** may demand. 1 blacksmith, 1 tailor, 1 seamstress, 1 tanner, 1 cooper, 2 wainwrights, 2 cobblers and 2 carpenters reside here. The cooper and carpenters share a workshop/home.

These folks accept work from strangers with coin, but only with the **Duke's** permission. Alternatively, a plan for surreptitious payment and delivery along with a significant bribe would probably work as well.

Greenslide Falls

Small logging camp whose inhabitants are meant to clear the land. Named after a slick and mossy cascade of small waterfalls a short distance upstream. Currently the project has a skeleton crew, actively stretching out this assignment far from their superiors for as long as possible.

Pasty & Pie

Serf village responsible for tending the huge wheat and barley fields to the south. Justifiably famous for the quality of its namesake. A reptile & peas pasty with an apple pie makes for one hell of a good meal. **The Count** has several dozen of both sent downstream to *Fort Deadfin* daily.

Lumber Beach

Logging camp sending tons of long, straight pine logs downstream every day along with barrels of wood ash (to make lye, potash, etc.) and jugs of pitch.

Fort Deadfin

Little more than a four story fortified home between two towers, from here **Count Joehaund Lizardbane** nervously rules. The northern wall contains a broad, shadowy portal back to Coldgrippe Duchy, behind a heavy portcullis. Every few days a wagon or two of County produce is carried back to the Duchy. Shipments going the other direction are significantly more infrequent.

Adventure 1: Humans Attack!!!

Towards the southern end of the *Wide River's* lake-like final bend, dozens of horrifying Human beings float aboard a fat keelboat, heading northeast. They've already seriously injured a young **Broomistega** girl. **Dean Longshell's** almost paranoid scrying proved to be invaluable. **The Dean** knew within minutes of an oar breaking the poor girl's ribs.

Longshell immediately whispered warnings to all traveling professors with whom he had a strong enough bond, though few were capable of whispering back across so many leagues. Of course, the dragonfly messengers were released to warn the land folk; swift **Acanthodes** sped through the waters to spread the word.

Still, it may be 2-3 days before a useful response can be mustered... longer, perhaps, for a coordinated response.

Something must be done!

After ordering his pearl handled fusils be brought up from the basement, **Dean Longshell** spun himself into moonbeams and flashed his way into *The Busted Barge*. Maybe it's best to fight Humans with Humans, or whatever strange creatures from foreign worlds happen to be about. If nothing else, it might buy the Paleozoic folks some time.

The Busted Barge

A long low building, constructed from the remnants of a derelict Golden Barge. The stools and tables are uncomfortably low to the ground, and the haphazardly fermented wine varies a great deal in viscosity and alcohol content. Still though, it's one of the few places in the Sphere where you can buy a drink, or buy anything at all. The Barge accepts both coin and barter.

The *Busted Barge Cooperative* is operated by 3 friendly blubberous **Ulemosaurs**, 2 leery **Xenacanths** and 1 chatty, venerable **Sphenacodon**.

Most of its regulars are Human students in **Dean Longshell's** new *Terrestrial-Marine Nautiloid Wizardry College*. However, the School is quite empty at the moment. Other than two apprentices quite sick with flu, the rest of the students and staff are currently touring the new *Ammonite Benthic University*.

The Deal

Dean Longshell is openly offering to cast "Agelessness" on anyone willing to confront the sudden Human menace. He provides 2 Fancy Fusils, 7 Plasmic Orbs and a Void Canoe (as a golden barge but it only seats 8 and you have to Flight Paddle) as both payment and equipage. "Agelessness" (pg 99) will only be cast upon the characters' return.

If that's not enough, he has 2 Experimental Grenades and a saltwater-pitted, golden statuette of a Faun mid-frolic to offer as well. These take 8 hours to summon because of the *Abyssal Crevice* in which they are stored — that's a significant delay.

Experimental Grenades — copper ovoids the size of a fat egg, activated by pressing 2 stiff levers on the top in opposite directions. Damage as Dragon-Fire (Troika! pg 76) in a 1d6x10' radius. On a fumble or if jarred, the grenade explodes right where it is — in someone's face, I bet.

Further, *Dean Longshell* continues to monitor the Humans and keeps the characters up to date on their actions... assuming one of the characters is willing to give him a tooth — magic is weird (he only senses instances of great fear or pain, and can only message infrequently).

Before parting to rally his people, *Longshell* emphatically expresses his belief that a violent solution to this problem will only result in more and worsening violence in the future.

It takes 12 hours of intense Flight Paddling to reach *Point 1* from *Terragyre*.

Also, *Sweet Teeth*, the elderly *Sphenacodon* vintner, is eager to go along, but she won't be ready until the following morning.

"There's a conversation I've gotta have with the stars, dearies. They're much too quiet during the day."

That's quite a bit more time for Humans to be terrible toward other innocents.

She is, however, a powerful Star Witch, capable of giving herself and allies supernatural vitality, but at the cost of literal years off her life. Currently, *Sweet Teeth* has 13 years remaining. Each Spell costs her not Stamina but rather 1d6 years of living. Should her years remaining go to zero, she dies when her Ferocior Form ceases in 3 days. If she has less than zero years remaining she dies immediately.

Ferocior Sweet Teeth
Skill: **10** *Stamina:* **18** *Initiative:* **2** *Damage as Large Beast*

ADVANCED SKILLS
1 Constellation Ferocior (pg 26)
1 Constellation of Vitality (pg 26)
1 Call the Voidstar Constellation (pg 26)

SPECIAL
Ferocior Sweet Teeth regenerates 2 Stamina every combat round. It takes her about 1 restful minute to regenerate fully, including severed limbs.

Who are the Humans? Why are they here now?

Sir Fredward Swordbloom, heir to landed knight **Sir Edard Swordbloom**, has managed to wheedle both a new title and charge from **Count Lizardbane**. He is now the "Grand Surveyor" and has been charged with "Exploration of the Wide River through to the Sea". He quickly gathered his 24-man levy and set out in *The Gutted Shark*, a keelboat with a small sail carrying far more beer and cider than strictly necessary.

Sir Fredward Swordbloom, Knight and Grand Surveyor

SKILL: 6 STAMINA: 7 INITIATIVE: 2 ARMOR: 3 DAMAGE AS FUSIL OR LONGSWORD

Greasy hair, greasy eyes, greasy words. *Sir Fredward* frequently splashes rosewater on his sweating, pink face. He hasn't taken off his fabulous floral-themed armor since the boat lost sight of the apple trees. The truth is he's terrified, and uses laudanum to mask his physical discomfort and fear. He feels he must live up to the drunken boasts that landed him this position. *Fredward* subscribes to the popular opinion that critters are not supposed to talk, and those that do are clearly DEMONS, WITCHES or DEMON-WITCHES.

Sir Staniel Gordson, Knight and Captain of the Gutted Shark

SKILL: 6 STAMINA: 8 INITIATIVE: 2 ARMOR: 1 DAMAGE AS FUSIL OR LONGSWORD

Older fellow with a well-etched sneer, graying at the temples, wrapped in an oiled cloak and well-worn leather armor. *Sir Staniel* recently acquired captainship of this vessel after remarking to *Count Lizardbane* on a new interest in nautical matters. He's the sort of fellow who welcomes violence with open arms.

ADVANCED SKILLS
-1 'Boat Stuff'

Rickarden, Count Lizardbane's Hunting Attendant

SKILL: 6 STAMINA: 9 INITIATIVE: 2 ARMOR: 0 DAMAGE AS FUSIL OR AXE

He was the very first soul levied for this quest. *Rick's* doing his best to remain positive, regardless of his circumstance. The pink-faced young man intends to keep a very keen eye on the lay of the land. If he can just convince *Marianna* to wed him, they can take the dowry goats and flee to the wilds, shrugging loose the fetterlocks of servitude.

ADVANCED SKILLS
2 Tracking
1 Stealth

Wallham and Kambert, Foresters of the South Range
Skill: **8** *Stamina:* **9** *Initiative:* **2** *Armor:* **0** *Damage as Fusil or Axe*

Two tanned and rugged fellows in surprisingly nice doublets, comfortably middle-aged. **Walham** has a wife back home, **Bell**; **Kambert** only has **Wallham**. **Kambert** is still a bit catty over **Bell**. Dragged from their isolated homes in the south of the *Apple Forest*, both men deeply resent this mission and personally despise **Sir Fredward**.

ADVANCED SKILLS
2 Forestry
2 Tracking
1 Stealth
1 Trapping

First Mate Aelfreadrick, former Captain of The Gutted Shark
Skill: **8** *Stamina:* **10** *Initiative:* **2** *Armor:* **0** *Damage as Fusil or Hammer*

With windswept hair and windswept, wrinkled skin, **Fread** grimaces with seething bile and anger always in his throat. He does the actual work of running the boat, along with his crew. The first mate would much rather crack **Sir Staniel's** skull open like a walnut and toss **Fredward**, armor and all, into the river's deep. For now **Fread** clenches his teeth and follows orders. He keeps a hollow mallet half-full of lead shot in his belt for knocking pegs and people back into place.

ADVANCED SKILLS
2 Boat Stuff
1 Fishing
1 Stealth

The Crew of the Gutted Shark

Skll:6 Stam:9 Init:2 Armr:0 Club/Knife

Jack — Lithe prankster, fiercely loyal to **Aelfreadrick** (1 Stealth, 1 Sleight of Hand).

Harold — friggin' **HUGE**, soft-hearted, loyal to **Aelfreadrick** (2 Strength).

Fran — Sturdy woman of few words, but her expressions speak volumes (2 Club Fighting, 1 Fishing, 1 Boatstuff).

Kathop — Akward and quiet fellow, new to the crew (3 Knife Fighting).

Porters

Skll:6 Stam:9 Init:2 Armr:0 Knife

Quindle — Faux-cheerful, hopes everyone gets eaten by "LIZARDS."

Jorten — Much too old for all this shit, probably napping if possible.

James — Usually dissociated, trembles whenever a voice gets raised, cries if the voice is pointed at him.

Quix — Always scheming, avoiding work and blaming others for his failings.

Hende — Courteous, attentive, tireless, and self-effacing. Favorite of the Sirs, disliked by most everyone else.

Dim — Pretends to be a mute simpleton, always on the lookout for a chance to get drunk and rowdy. Only **Quindle, Jorten** and **James** know the truth.

Quix — Focusing on learning to juggle right now. She secretly wants to slip back through the Portal and join the circus (0 Juggling).

Jeffers — Hopelessly addicted to dice, jonesing terribly for a gambling fix. Nobody on board trusts him or his loaded dice.

Vivian — Meek. Lover of animals, deeply upset by the "river lizard girl" being hurt by **Sir Fredward**.

Loggers (levied to act as Soldiers)
Skll:6 Stam:9 Init:2 Armr:0 Spear

Guym — Hairy, surly, usually drunk (2 Bar Brawling).

Brayst — Lanky, lethargic crosscut saw man.

Svaren — Short, bubbly other half of the crosscut saw team.

Breen — Chubby, bombastic and foolhardy older man.

Niq — Always volunteers to go it alone. Would prefer to have stayed forever in the woods she knows and loves.

Quanta — Very disturbed by *Sir Fredward's* casual violence towards a defenseless creature just asking some questions.

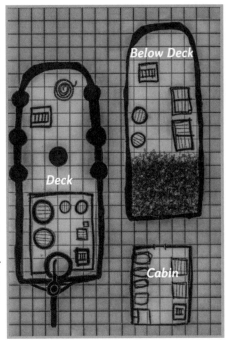

Swineherds
(levied to act as Soldiers)
Skll:6 Stam:8 Init:2 Armr:0 Spear

Timerthy — Boisterous and young, eager to please, true believer in the divine right of the ruling class.

Mystern — He's mostly just happy to be at something else other than chasing pigs around the woods.

Shundt — Born rabble rouser, quick with a helping hand and a joke at the expense of his "betters."

Bruce — Long ago resigned to his lot in life, he refuses to fight for or against his fate.

Bernetadine — An excessive fountain of jubilation and wonder, she's doing her best not to be brought down by the glum world she inhabits.

MEMBERS OF THE EXPEDITION WHO WILL NEVER NEGOTIATE WITH THESE "MONSTERS"
Sir Fredward Swordbloom, incompetent, vain, craven expedition leader.
Sir Staniel Gordson, sadistic captain of *The Gutted Shark*.
Hende, overly courteous porter.
Breen, bombastic graying logger.
Timerthy, kowtowing swineherd.

MEMBERS UNLIKELY TO NEGOTIATE WITH THESE "CRITTERS" UNLESS COERCED OR BRIBED
Aelfreadrick, resentful former captain, now first mate.
Jack, prankster very loyal to **Aelfreadrick**.
Harold, big softie, remaining much too loyal to **Aelfreadrick**.
Niq, logger who just wants to get back to wandering her woods.
Guym, drunk and surly logger.
Mystern, mildly enthusiastic swineherd.
Bruce, resigned swineherd.

Wallham, forester unhappy to be away from his home and wife.
Kambert, forester glad to have *Wallham* "to himself."
Rickarden, hunting attendant desperate to start a new life in the wilds.
Fran, woman of few words and searing looks, member of the boat crew.
Kathop, awkward fellow and former knife thrower in a circus.
Quindle, insincerely upbeat porter.
Jorten, sleepy and elderly porter.
James, detachedly anxious porter.
Quix, lazy and scheming porter.
Dim, porter pretending to be a complete simpleton.
Quix, porter wishing she could join the circus.
Jeffers, gambling addicted porter
Vivian, animal lover and porter.
Brayst, tall lethargic logger.
Svaren, short and perky logger.
Quanta, logger who's deeply uncomfortable with violence.
Shundt, swineherd and firebrand.
Bernetadine, trying to stay upbeat despite being a conscripted swineherd.

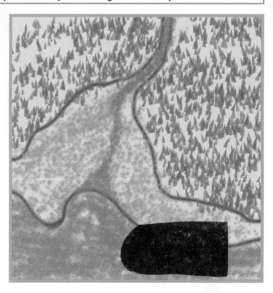

Timeline of Human Actions (assuming no interference)

Day 1

- ⊕ *Late Morning, Point 1:* **Sir Fredward** breaks a **Broomistega** girl's ribs with an oar because she dared to speak to him.

- ⊕ *Early Afternoon: The Gutted Shark* sails just north of *Gold Stone Island* but dares not come ashore.

- ● *Evening, Point 2:* the HUMANS take the boat ashore and open several casks of cider. Most are rip-roaring drunk by Late Evening.

Day 2

- ⊕ *Early Morning, Point 2:* the hungover expedition is attacked by 6 **Dimetrodons** from a local clan. The synapsids, having heard of their violence towards other creatures, vigorously defend their territory. The HUMANS are driven away without casualty, leaving behind 2 casks of cider and several tents. Only 3 **Dimetrodons** survive the encounter.

- ⊕ *Mid Morning:* while sailing once more past *Gold Stone Island*, the HUMANS are confronted by a pair of **Accord Keepers**. The two **Xenacanths** formally demand the expedition leave **Queen Brightspine's** sovereign territory. They're answered with fusil fire, but there are no further casualties. *6 Accord Keepers* keep close tabs on *The Gutted Shark* from below until the water turns too brackish.

- ● *Evening, Point 3:* after a hard day at the oars, *The Gutted Shark* drops anchor near the southwest beach of *Silthead Island*. They don't notice the nearby multi-species village of *Silthome*, just inland over a low ridge.

- ● *Midnight:* an interconnected series of bonfires along the beach are set ablaze by locals, effectively creating a wall of fire between the boat and the village. In a panic the HUMANS sail blind for nearly an hour before dropping anchor for a pitch black and sleepless night.

Day 3

⊕ *Early Morning, Point 4:* the **Humans** head toward shore as soon as dawn touches the sky. There they scout for fresh water, the tide having turned the river too brackish. The porters are ordered to complete this task unaccompanied, much to their chagrin. However, **Walham** and **Kambert** voluntarily join the porters. It takes until noon to fill two hogsheads.

⊕ – ⊕ *All Afternoon:* The Gutted Shark circles around *Terragyre Isle* as quickly as possible. Beneath them, potential destruction awaits: underwater wizards and fanciful magical constructs and gigantic enchanted Helicoprions, oh my! All tensely wait for the **Humans** to do, well, almost anything. The expedition for the most part huddles inside the cabin the entire time.

● *Evening:* The winds change as *The Gutted Shark* completes its transit around the island. **Fread** points the boat towards the midpoint of *Terragyre* and *Silthome*, wishing to be as far as possible away from them both. They drop anchor and endure another overcast and lightless night.

Days 4-5

The **Humans** sail back to their county as quickly as they possibly can.

But remember: this is the timeline with no interference. The experience **Humans** have if unmolested is sufficient for **The Count** to request his father, **Duke Coldegrippe**, to call in his levies next winter. **The Duke** delays this at least another year. However, if the perceived threat of the "demon territories" is exacerbated, or if the large, well-armed expedition doesn't return, **Duke Coldegrippe** is likely to grant his son's request.

The end result largely depends on who (if anyone) returns and what they've witnessed. For instance, if only sympathetic expedition members return, they may be able to convince **Count Lizardbane** that the expansion of *County Lizardbane* must be handled slowly. This gives the *Wide River Valley* nations time to bolster their defenses, and even possibly pursue diplomatic resolutions.

The Count remains torn between a great fear of not conquering the valley in a timely fashion and the terror of reporting any sort of self-perceived loss to his **Father**.

Adventure 2: Voids of the Less Indifferent Stars
Part 1: "Stones Below, Stars Above"

Dimetrodon Territory

Dimetrodon Matriarch Runway Cuddles (yes, *that* **Runway Cuddles**) of the **Sunnystone Fashion Clan** had a very unpleasant extrasensory experience while sunning in her favorite late afternoon spot. Had she noticed the Evening Stars spelling out both the Crooked Grin and the Sunning Fool, she certainly wouldn't have been snoring a bit on the central dais just then...

In her defense, Runway's grandniece, **Quick Fan**, was insisting on dressing like a flower bush. **Runway** herself wears flowers more often than not. She pioneered their use in high fashion, in fact, but flowers are accessories. A floral tiara, an elaborate corsage on the tip of one's tail: there are many bold ways to use flowers without looking so ridiculous or making such a mess. That young synapsid had been dusting everything in petals, all day long. **Quick Fan's** father, **Sunshine Bathe**, would not stop complaining. It really was distracting.

When she should have been focused on her breathing and the slowly fading warmth of the basalt beneath her, instead she was assaulted by a deep cold of still waters, where nothing happens save slow decay. She felt all at once dozens of terrains underneath her tired feet. In her mind's unwitting eye she saw indistinct statues below the very stones on which she rested. About the indistinct soapstone figures swam living darkness.

This was several days ago.

It really has been a bother: anxiously waiting for travelers so that she might entice them to explore underneath the amphitheater. The Stars put something down there, or maybe they just noticed something down there. They clearly want some travelers to go poke around. What else could all the different terrains mean?

The Stars must be kept entertained. If that means **Runway** must use her considerable talents to act as Stage Manager to Adventure, then so be it!

Runway Cuddles offers: THANKS, a FABULOUS BANQUET, FASHIONABLE CLOTHES, FASHION SCENE CONTACTS and a GOLD AND AQUAMARINE BRACELET she was gifted ages ago. She claims the bracelet was found in the cave if she thinks that will help. (**Runway** can make designs for ALL sorts of body shapes and sizes. She spent two seasons in *Terragyre* and met a multitude of folks).

The Hole Beneath the Amphitheater

The *Sunnystone Fashion Amphitheater* was built atop a large slate sheet set into a flaking shale hillside. Beneath that big gray flagstone lies a void, burrowed by some ancient thing some unknown time ago.

A hole into the void has been dug in front of the stage, into which hangs a RICKETY ROPE LADDER leading to the center of *Room A*.

13 minutes after characters enter *Rooms A* or *B* in this complex, one COLD SHADOW TANGLE [*Skll:7 Stam:6 Init:2 Armr:0*] (pg 79) rises up from the frigid earth for each sentient, corporeal being present. Leaving and reentering causes more TANGLES to arise. They descend back into the earth after 1 day of not interacting with living things.

TANGLES generally mill about the room's entrances/exits and attempt to touch anyone getting within a dozen or so feet of them. Their only real senses are of touch and the flavor of bio-electric magnetic fields (the delicious taste of living energy/potential).

Should more than 27 TANGLES be present in *A* or *B*, the room COLLAPSES in 3d6 minutes. It is readily apparent the COLLAPSE is imminent.

The TANGLES restore the room to its former dimensions in 1d6 days, slowly pushing the collapsed ceiling into place.

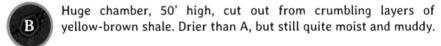

A Characters drop down from the hole above (X). Along the southern edge a large, cold puddle slowly drains down through scratchy gravel and muck. All the while, water seeps in through the wet walls. There is no discernible structure holding up the soft mud and flaking rock walls. An occasional drip punctuates the damp darkness.

On the northern edge of this area a hole leads *Down and East* and while a tunnel leads *Up and North*. There is also a *Pale Blue Door* on the eastern edge of the *Up and North* tunnel. (Note here that *Up* and *Down* are elevations.)

Down and East: climbing into the damp, gravely hole leads one through a long, dark, winding tunnel, eventually opening into B before continuing on to C, all the while getting notably tighter the closer one gets to C.

Up and North: this long, wide tunnel goes for almost 1,500' in a long curve, eventually coming out at C.

Pale Blue Door: a small retinal scanner on the left side of this door opens for no one currently living. The door itself is made of self-healing plastic, set 12" into the surrounding wall. Cuts and the like, basically Damage that doesn't remove a chunk, close back up in 1d3 minutes. Gaps of more than two fingers' width cannot be closed. Behind the door is a short tunnel to B.

B Huge chamber, 50' high, cut out from crumbling layers of yellow-brown shale. Drier than A, but still quite moist and muddy.

C After the long *Up and North* tunnel finally curves southward for several hundred feet, it abruptly switchbacks to head almost due north again, truncating before an ALABASTER ARCHWAY. Inside the ARCHWAY, pinpoints of light flit about, briefly pausing to form CONSTELLATIONS.

Some are recognizable, while some look familiar but cannot be placed in memory. Still, some others look like nervous nausea in a way immediately recognizable but difficult to explain.

The ARCHWAY leads to room G on the *Moon Surface Complex* (pg 50).

D ⊛ Gray soapstone statue of a highly-stylized, bipedal figure tensely kneeling; its identifiable features are abstracted into a minimal number of smooth surfaces. Around its neck hangs a SILVER COMPASS WITH A COPPER NEEDLE AND GOLDEN CHAIN. The needle always points to the entrance to *Wonder Claw's Dig* (pg 58).

E ⊛ Gray-green soapstone mural quadrant, mounted to a gray slate wall. This is a large, fully functional ASTRONOMICAL INSTRUMENT. Looking through its sight, one can see the stars as though it were a clear and cloudless night.

This is true even here, underground, and remains true so long as the wall to which it is mounted remains parallel to a north-south meridian. The wall is currently set quite firmly in place.

F ⊛ Bas-relief sculpture of a starry sky, painstakingly carved from a huge cube of snowflake obsidian. Each white fleck on the northern surface protrudes slightly, the black ground having been carefully cut away. It usually takes several moments for the intent of the piece to come through.

Some constellations are recognizable, specifically: THE CONSTELLATION OF WISDOM, THE TWIN-TAILED WORM, THE SHUNNED STAR and THE CONQUEROR ON THE BEAST'S BACK.

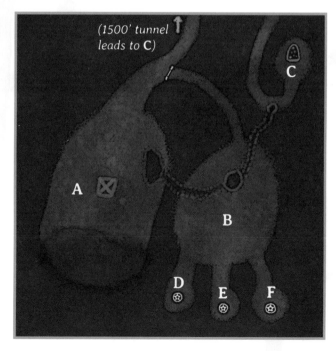

(1500' tunnel leads to **C**)

The Moon Surface Complex

The air is dry and thin now, and frigid. The walls and ceiling are made of a matte black, thick plastic, with neon lights like wainscotting humming in malachite green. The faint smell of ozone feels pregnant, but nothing comes of it except for static cling.

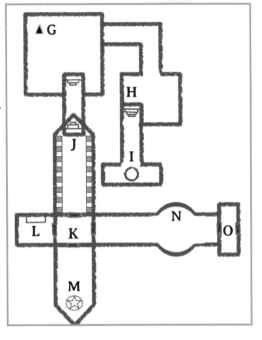

Near the northwest corner: the portal back to C is on this end a golden equilateral triangle filled with swirling shadows.

On the east wall: a black plastic door, noticeable only by an absence of electric wainscotting. It has been seamlessly sealed shut and requires significant force to break it down.

On the south wall: a staircase descends into a short hall with alabaster walls, leading to an ascending staircase to room J.

The matte black plastic continues down the hall until reaching a glossy black curtain, behind which is a square room. The north wall is alabaster. The other 3 walls are gigantic glass screens displaying looping video images!

On the west wall: several scenes of stylized, bipedal figures proudly zipping through starry skies in strange ships. In one of the scenes a moon-like ship heads towards a planet with a jagged red slash through it.

On the south wall: a single, looping scene of the stylized figures being chastised by animate and unfamiliar constellations formed from red stars.

On the east wall: the stylized figures huddle in pleading shame, reaching skyward. The constellations turn towards them and shift from red to violet and finally to blue, at which point the beseeching figures dissolve into clouds of tiny stars.

In the southwest corner: stairs descend to another alabaster hallway.

The hall dead ends in a wide, shallow room thrumming with intense SOUND WAVES below the range of HUMAN and critter hearing: it can be felt through the vibrating floor. Combined with the INTENSE SMELL of off gassing plastics, this room is a nauseous place to be.

In the room's center is a circular pad of polished metal. If stepped on, STAR SERVANT, PENITENT-17 [SKLL:*10* STAM:*20* INIT:*4* ARMR:*3 (2 vs energy attacks)*] (pg 54) phases in through the ceiling.

On the east wall: a whiteboard with flaking diagrams and calculations scrawled all over it. With sufficient time, the Mathmologically inclined may be able to deduce this room is a *TELEPORTATION MACHINE*! A dried-out dry erase marker and eraser sit on the bottom ledge.

On the west wall: a dizzying array of colorful buttons and dials is set into the polished white wall. Touching any of these controls causes STAR SERVANT, PENITENT-17 to phase in from the ceiling.

Stairs lead up into a much wider hallway of green and blue marble floors, padded beige walls and white luminescent ceilings.

Running along the walls, for the entire length of the hall, are 16 glass display cases, each featuring the skeletons of a different species of primate, 8 on either side. Connecting each case is a 2' high oaken table.

On the south wall: a door is set into the center. It slides open when approached, closing several moments later.

NOTE: In rooms J-N there is a 1-in-6 chance to encounter the 3 VARANOPS ZOMBIE-BOYS: *Scritch, Scratch* and *Bite* [SKLL:*5* STAM:*7* INIT:*2* ARMR:*1*] (pg 55).

If they've yet to be encountered by the time the characters reach *Room N* they are there, probably arguing about the exact coloration of a pretty girl they used to know.

K Padded beige walls, marbled floors and luminescent ceilings continue. There are 4 sliding doors, one on each wall, with large green and red buttons to the right, as well as a labeled 9-button keypad on the left. If more than 10 incorrect attempts to unlock a door are made within 10 minutes, the door locks from both sides and does not unlock without an *ADMINISTRATOR'S BADGE*. The doors are VERY sturdy. There's a 1" gap between the bottom of the door and the floor. There are several tears in the beige padding along the very bottom of the walls.

On the north wall: an unlocked door leading to J. On this side it opens when the green button is pressed and locks when the red button is pressed. The unlock code 2-4-6-8 has been written in marker above the keypad.

On the east wall: a locked door leading to N. The unlock code is 0-1-0-1. Like the northern door, it automatically opens from the other side. It closes after 10 seconds with no one in the way.

On the south wall: a locked door leading to M. The unlock code is 0-0-0-1. Like the northern door, it automatically opens from the other side. It closes after 10 seconds with no one in the way.

On the west wall: a locked door leading to L. The unlock code is 1-3-5-7. "1-3-5-" followed by an indecipherable smudge is scrawled above the keypad. This door automatically opens from the other side and closes after 10 seconds.

L Another hallway, this one ending with a glass screen on which the *STAR DUNGEONS MAP* is displayed.

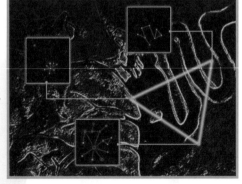

A wide, padded bench protrudes from the *north wall.* An *ADMINISTRATOR'S BADGE* is attached to the underneath of it by crumbling plastic tape. The *BADGE* is a 4"×4" plastic card with a 5 pointed green star printed on it. If touched to a keypad, the door unlocks and the keys light up in the order of the unlock code.

If examined closely there is a thin 4" wide slot at the bottom of the glass screen. Should an *ADMINISTRATOR'S BADGE* be inserted the screen switches to a live satellite feed of the *Wide River Valley.* Onscreen controls allow one to zoom and scroll about. It can't get high enough resolution to identify specific individuals, but the movements of living things can be seen.

Another hallway, this one truncating in a triangular alcove. A 4' tall, solid silver statue of a refracting telescope stands a few feet in front of the alcove, with a broad, snowflake obsidian base.

In the very back of the alcove: a small, red, plastic flashlight with 12 hours of battery remaining.

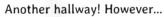 Another hallway! However...

 At the midpoint of this hallway is a perfect sphere, composed of completely transparent force of will. It is unyielding, immovable and nearly indestructible. It allows passage only via the hallway which enters and exits the sphere.

The sphere itself is ¾ buried in pale gray rocks and sand. The sky above reveals familiar constellations, but far too bright and showing hundreds of stars, too dim to see from the planet's surface.

On the east wall: a locked door leading to O. It only opens with an ADMINISTRATOR'S BADGE present. Even so, when the green button is pressed the entire door pulses with red light three times. It must be pressed again before it slides dolorously open.

This is a repeat of the beige walls and illuminated ceilings found in K, with large green and red buttons and a keypad, though the floor is bare concrete. The door leading in does not automatically close.

On the east wall: another door, this one sullenly glowing red already.

When the GREEN BUTTON is pressed once the door glows more brightly.

When the GREEN BUTTON is pressed twice the door glows more brightly and then slams shut.

When the GREEN BUTTON is pressed thrice the door opens to the surface of an atmosphereless moon. Everyone is now DROWNING.

The complex itself seems to be mostly buried underneath an enormous mound of rubble. Probably everyone dies before they get to see that, though.

When the RED BUTTON is pressed the lock resets, and if open, the exit door closes and the entry door opens.

On the south wall: a fishbowl type ASTRONAUT HELMET hangs from a hook.

On the north wall: a black, POLYESTER BACKPACK hangs from a hook. It's in surprisingly good condition.

Star Servant, Penitent-17

SKILL 10
STAMINA 20
INITIATIVE 4
ARMOUR 3 (2 vs energy attacks)
DAMAGE as Large Beast

	MIEN
1	Cold, Bored, and Hungry
2	Bored, Cold, and Hungry
3	Hungry, Bored, and Cold
4	Deeply Sleeping
5	Cold, Sleeping
6	Sleeping, Cold

An 8' tall being composed of hundreds of slowly swirling miniature stars in the vague shape of a humanoid. They have been tasked with ensuring this teleportation pad (*TELEPAD*) is never used to allow anyone onto or off of the planet below. They really don't want to hurt anyone, but moreso they wish for this long penance to be over.

They might be convinced to operate the telepad so as to send the party back down to the planet. The party came from the planet, after all. Doing so materializes the party on the roof of **Dean Longshell's** home in *Terragyre*.

Varanops Zombies: Scritch, Scratch & Bite

Skill 5
Stamina 7
Initiative 1
Armour 1
Damage as Small Beast

	Mien
1	Cold, Bored, and Hungry
2	Bored, Cold, and Hungry
3	Hungry, Bored, and Cold
4	Deeply Sleeping
5	Cold, Sleeping
6	Sleeping, Cold

These small, 3' long undead synapsids have been here for a few million years, and they've been cold and hungry the entire time. The warmth of blood is a hard thing to resist. It takes all of their stoogely cunning to get some.

Varanops are shaped like a sideways comma or a tadpole, if either of those things had four sprawling legs and a pointy mouth full of sharp little teeth. These boys, being very old zombies, have flesh like flaking cardboard beneath leathery skin. Their bones are still perfectly strong. The three are hard to distinguish. However, Scritch has a long string tied to his tail, with a pebble on the other end, and Scratch has a small scar on his forehead.

Special
When sleeping they appear to be nothing more than desiccated corpses.

Part 2: "Soil and Shame"

Within the Giant Berm Northeast of Shadepool

Some time ago*, a particularly crotchety old **Thrinaxodon, Wonder Claw**, decided she was just plain, damn fed up with everyone. She even resigned her *Shadepool* citizenship with a formal Declarative Log. She then spent the better part of two weeks tirelessly digging out a deep, complicated burrow. The few members of her family who tried to visit claimed she hadn't had that much energy in ages.

After another week, she came stumbling into her son's burrow, shaking and gray. Her flesh was cold to the touch. After sleeping for 2 days she awoke and could neither remember leaving the community nor her time in the burrows.

Wonder Claw passed away 11 years ago. None of her relatives survived, either. However, her Declarative Log is still available in the *Mayor's Filing Room*.

Basically everyone in and around *Shadepool* knows the **Wonder Claw** story by heart. Many could even lead the way to the entrance. Most won't, though.

More often than not, ghosts are pegged as the danger in *Wonder Claw's Dig*, though skeleton monsters, hideous Human-Thrinaxodon chimeras and cannibal Broomistegas are also popular theories.

The Declarative Log

Mayor Budding Stillness (Broomistega) really doesn't have time to help anyone investigate. Their partner and assistant, **Lumen Cheer (Thrinaxodon)**, is out today. They are quite curious about the Log, and only ask that the characters leave it on their ornately carved desk after it's found. There are only 40 or so Logs in the Renunciation stack, it's relatively easy to find.

It reads:

> "I, Wonder Claw, do hereby renounce my citizenship to Shadepool, effective immediately and forever. For the Stars must be kept amused. The Conqueror on the Beast's Back has become blood and pain in the conqueror's wake. Past the Portal into the Sky there is the map. At the third point the Conqueror may be inverted, that the conqueror's End might be made."

*Sources disagree, but this all went down 16 years ago.

---

* Sources disagree, but this all went down 16 years ago.

D6	Encounters Atop the Berm
1	**Whittley Floof (Thrinaxodon)** is the Infrastructure Inspector. Every day he checks on the *Berm* and other large bits of infrastructure about the burrow city for signs of failure. He'll warn everyone away from *Wonder Claw's Dig,* but is willing to indicate its general location "over 'round about the trees."
2	Odd dots of thick fog, a few feet wide and several feet high, form a winding line leading directly to *Wonder Claw's Dig.*
3	Several dozen **Broomistega Youths** are carrying oiled sacks of river water and dragonfly larvae across the *Berm* on their way to the *aquaculture burrows,* south of town. They don't have much time, but nervously point the way to *Wonder Claw's Dig.*
4	A cold, fierce wind blows in from the southeast. A wild flock of giant dragonflies takes refuge in the trees and bushes on the *Berm's* southern end.
5	The cloudless, whitewashed sky is particularly empty atop the *Berm.*
6	Small rocks have been arranged into a frowny face on a patch of bare ground atop the *Berm.*

The *Berm* itself ranges from 50-80' high, is 200-300' wide and more than half a mile long. Its northern tip is mostly bare soil and stone; there, dozens of workers (**Ulemosaurs, Thrinaxodons** and **Broomistegas**) carefully add unwanted stones and soil. The rest is covered in short scratchy grasses, with a few conifers growing on the much older southern end.

Wonder Claw's Dig

In a copse of resinous conifers with morosely dangling, strap-like leaves, a short, stacked stone wall holds open the entrance to *Wonder Claw's Dig*. Yellow, uncut stone stairs lead into the darkness below. In the burrow the air is cold and dry.

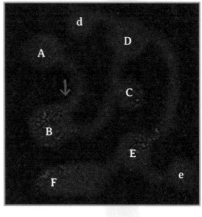

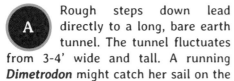 Rough steps down lead directly to a long, bare earth tunnel. The tunnel fluctuates from 3-4' wide and tall. A running **Dimetrodon** might catch her sail on the wooden support beams while an **Ulemosaurus** has to crawl carefully through.

There is a bit of a nook to the west of the bottom step. In it lies the mostly decomposed body of a **Thrinaxodon**. If disturbed she rises up as a Shame Ghost of the Friendless Dead (pg 60). Otherwise she remains sleeping for a few seasons yet.

B The tunnel opens into a 12' wide, 17' tall conical room held open by a teepee-like lattice of lashed-together logs. 2 Shame Ghosts of the Friendless Dead [Skll:10 Stam:5 Init:1 Armr:2] (pg 60) rest on the southern side of the heavy central support pillar, sleeping during the day. At night they rise up and float about the small room, keening.

C More of a large nook than a proper room, this void is half the height of the tunnel and unsupported. It could easily collapse. 2 Shame Ghosts of the Friendless Dead [Skll:10 Stam:5 Init:1 Armr:2] (pg 60) are tucked into the veeery back.

D Another 12'×17' conical room containing a 4'×2' chest with 2 separately opening, square compartments. 5 decorative holes have been drilled into the northern edge of the chest, 4 on the southern.

The left compartment is unmarked. It contains an *ISOSCELES TRIANGLE, 12" WIDE AND 17" LONG, MADE OF THICK, CONTINUOUS GOLDEN WIRE.* When touched to an unhappy spirit, said spirit is immediately banished unto the aether. This makes it handy for dispelling ghosts, but useless against devils and their insurmountable self esteem.

The right compartment is marked by a 9-pointed starburst. Opening it causes a brief and intense flash of SOLAR RADIATION. This probably blinds everyone nearby, as per Flash (Troika! pg 61). It also deals 1d6 Damage in the form of BLISTERING SUNBURNS. Roll Damage for each affected character. Make the players roll their own Damage, just to keep things quick (and a little mean).

2 Shame Ghosts of the Friendless Dead [*Skll:10 Stam:5 Init:1 Armr:2*] (pg 60) lie near the southern edge of this small, adjacent room.

Seven glowing orbs hang in place, around 1' from the floor, arranged in a horizontally flipped version of the Shunned Star constellation. The orbs can be laboriously moved by a living creature's hand.

The Shunned Star orb is in the center of this room. If the *Shunned Star* is moved into *Room E*, the floor on the western half of *Room F* glows indigo. If the other stars are all moved into *Room E*, the floor on the western half of *Room F* glows indigo AND all unattached Shame Ghosts dissolve into the aether.

This room retains the 3' height of the tunnels, but widens to 6½'. Five log pillars have been set into the north wall, while four are set into the south wall. In the center of the western half, a 4'×4'×2" basalt tablet is buried a few inches beneath loose dirt.

A crude and stylized version of the *Star Dungeons Map* (pg 52) has been carved on it. All throughout the eastern half of this room the soil is warm to the touch, getting rapidly warmer in seemingly random directions.

Bits of the dismembered Celestial Serpent Constellation [*Skll:16 Stam:32 Init:8 Armr:4 Gigantic Beast*] (as Dragon, Troika! pg 76) have been buried haphazardly here. There it waits until the first serpent evolves, then it may join its brethren in the sky, a long penance finally ended.

Every few minutes spent digging around on this side results in a 1-in-6 chance to uncover a piece of the Celestial Serpent, thus releasing it!

Once released, it sticks around for 1d6 combat rounds and probably tries to kill everyone. It begins about the size of a large anaconda and slowly expands from there. If treated with exaggeratedly worshipful respect, the Celestial Serpent might well go on its way to the sky peacefully.

Once released, 6% of all lizards spontaneously mutate into snakes, and a new constellation takes its place in the sky. No one takes this as a good sign.

Even fewer take the chain of stars darting out from the southern end of the *Berm* as anything but a monstrous omen. **Mayor Budding Stillness** has a very difficult time keeping the city from evacuating in a blind panic.

Shame Ghosts of the Friendless Dead
SKILL **10** *STAMINA* **5** *INITIATIVE* **1** *ARMOUR* **2**

DAMAGE ROLL➡	1	2	3	4	5	6	7+
Cold Fire of Shame	3	5	7	9	11	13	21

For the past seventeen years, those dying of illness in *Shadepool*, alone and without love, have leapt from their death beds and ran into the night, compelled to die in *Wonder Claw's Dig*. There they fitfully sleep until they rot to only bones. Their skulls then arise each night to pitifully moan, each alone in their presumably eternal torment.

	MIEN*
1	Morose
2	Lamenting Inconsolably
3	Needy
4	Resigned
5	Desperate
6	Dejected

Each skull rests on a pillar of starry teal fog, turning red when enraged. They can move with all the speed of a well thrown dart. They do not remember their names, nor any part of their history. They can speak, but elsewise they know nothing save their stunning need. Disturbing the ghost's remains causes them to rise up as well.

Special
SHAME GHOSTS want, more than anything, a friendly embrace. If expressly denied a hug they attack. If diverted or delayed, there's 10-20 minute window before they MUST know an answer (perhaps 30 minutes if tactfully handled).

D3	IF ALLOWED TO HUG A CHARACTER:
1	Character immediately loses 1d6 Stamina. The screaming cold of the abandoned dead is extremely unhealthy for the living to accept.
2	For the next minute the embrace can be ended. This is how long it takes the skull to embed into someone, after which the Stamina loss becomes permanent. Removed skulls immediately attack.
3	Character gains 1 Armour from the permanent, protective embrace. An ethereal, azure fog hangs about them from dusk until dawn.

Should anyone suggest the ghosts hug each other, seeing as they have so much in common, they most certainly will. This renders them once again inert, lifeless skulls.

---

*These are just a starting point. The Friendless Dead "match energy."

Part 3: "Starry Cave of the Inverted Conqueror"
Unclaimed Territory

D6	Encounter Chart for Surrounding Countryside. Roll 2/Day
1	Hot, dry gusts of petulant wind from the east.
2	Cooler, flirting breezes from the west.
3	Brief rainstorm followed by intense sunshine and steamy fog.
4	*Ulemosaur Merchant*, surprised to see anyone around here, hauling jars of coniferous resin.
5	1D3 Sauroctonus Jerks. If 2 are present they are a mated pair. If 3 are present 2 are a mated pair and 1 their child.
6	1D3 Young, Resentful Inostravencias.

On the east side of a dark rocky hill, in the back of a smallish cave, there waits a broad, circular hole. This nearly vertical shaft descends for almost 200'. The walls of the shaft itself, and all branching tunnels below, are covered in conical, stone spikes of random sizes and angles. A very faint, red-orange glow can be discerned from somewhere deep below. Climbing down this shaft for 60' requires a successful Climb Test, and takes one to the tippy top of the map (pg 62). From this point on, thick layers of lichen and moss grow everywhere.

Going from the top of map to a *Marked Location* or from one *Marked Location* to another requires a successful Climb Test with these exceptions: getting to rooms C or D requires you first go to room B, and getting to room H requires you first go to room G. This Test also allows the character to move about the ending location as needed.

Failing a Climb Test here causes a character to FALL TO THE BOTTOM of their starting *Marked Location*, suffering the Damage listed.

If the climb started at the top of map the falling character must Test Luck or die. If successful, they still take 3D6 Damage. There's a lot of water at the bottom, but also a number of spikes.

If a Climb Test is failed with double 6s, add +3 to total Damage rolled. Landing with a spike directly in them tender vittles, typical, innit?

Characters take ½ Damage (round down) if they are tied to an *ANCHORED ROPE*.

If a character has Climb as an Advanced Skill (or an equivalent), after 4 successful Tests they may move freely here.

What's Actually Going On Here?

The Stars that dwell in the Voidsea of this small backwater in the hump-backed sky have set bounds on this Sphere so that this novelty of a peaceful world might amuse them for ages.

Already — after merely a few billion years — dozens of Stars have turned their attention and ministrations elsewhere. Thus was the spontaneous connection to *Coldgrippe Duchy* made possible (as well as the opening in the sky above *Terragyre*).

The less indifferent Stars, in their broad but finite wisdom, took great pains to subtly empower the native folks against the rising threat of HUMANITY. These locations are their final and most direct action against the conquering COUNT. The unexpected presence of the **Men in the Moon-ship** simply made their aims easier to execute.

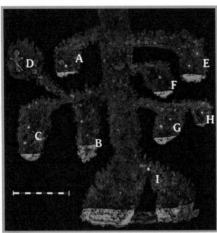

Light Orbs

In all but one of the *Marked Locations* (1-3), RED-TO-ORANGE GLOWING ORBS float inconveniently in the center of the room. It takes a negligible amount of force to move these around, but only if the force applied is intentional. The orbs stay exactly where they're at whenever a character stops applying force. They glow with the equivalent light of a bright, clean lantern.

 1 RED LIGHT ORB, 1-2' of Water, 2d6 FALLING DAMAGE.

 2 RED ORBS, 4-6' of Water, 3d6 FALLING DAMAGE. "Beware! That which is wrought here cannot be undone!!" shouts a staticky voice from *Location D*.

 2 RED ORBS, 1 Orange Orb, 2-3' of Water, 4d6 FALLING DAMAGE.

ANCHORED STAR PERSON EXPATRIATE, UNREPENTANT-23 [SKLL:*9* STAM:*18* INIT:*1* ARMR:*2* MODEST BEAST] (pg 64) speaks warnings. Unless crawling along the walls, this cavern can be explored without risk of falling if one is at the top of *Location B*.

2 Red Orbs, 2-3' of Water, 2d6 Falling Damage.

 1 Red Orb, 1-2' of Water, 2d6 Falling Damage.

 1 Red Orb, 2 Orange Orbs, 1-2' of Water, 3d6 Falling Damage.

 1 Orange Orb, 1' of Water, 1d6 Falling Damage.

 Bottom-most cavern, 3d6 Falling Damage. 14 conical stone pillars with flat tops project from 6-8' Water. 1 Red Orb sits atop the central most pillar, only a few feet from the cavern ceiling. The other 13 pillars only break the water's surface by a few feet.

Those familiar with Astrology might recognize The Conqueror on the Beast's Back. If all Light Orbs are placed 1 each atop a pillar, the Conqueror Constellation disappears from the sky, **Count Joehaund Lizardbane** dies and the Portal to *Coldgrippe Duchy* closes. This throws the Humans trapped here into disarray as those desiring authority contend with one another.

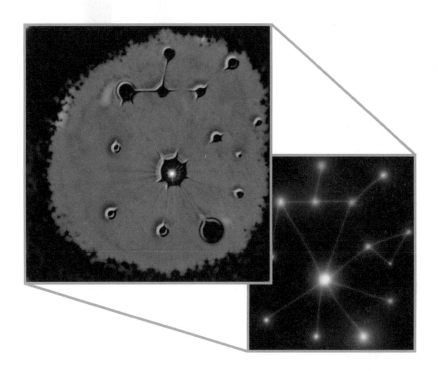

Anchored Star Person Expatriate, Unrepentant-23

SKILL 9
STAMINA 18
INITIATIVE 1
ARMOUR 2 (1 vs energy attacks)
DAMAGE as Modest Beast

	MIEN
1	Begging
2	Needing
3	Mournful
4	Wailing
5	Raging
6	Confused

3' pillar topped by a vaguely humanoid head and torso, built from swirling clouds of red to yellow starlight. They cannot move from this spot. They do not remember their name. They do not remember who they were or why they hate the Stars so.

Over the past eons of their confinement, all that has survived is their aggrievement against the Stars that damned them here.

Warnings thwart the masters' aims — they remember that much. What is done here cannot be undone. This is all they know. This is all they have become.

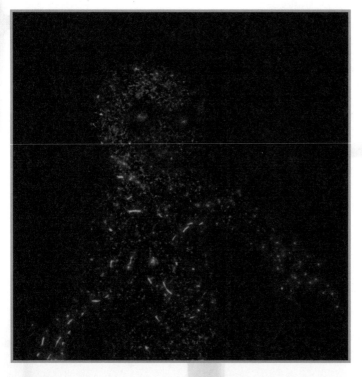

Random Village Charts

Whenever a village is indicated, note it down on y'alls campaign map. Generally assume these villages are composed of the species in the nation's name, except that most villages on the northern beach of the *Thrinaxodon and Broomistega Allied Protectorates* are **Ammonite** Communities.

"Day's walk" represents 6-8 hours of steadily walking across rough terrain, approximately 15-20 miles as the dragonfly flies. Assume 30-40 miles if all members of the party are in the sky.

D6	WHERE'S THE NEXT VILLAGE?
1	1 Day's Walk Northish.
2	2 Day's Walk Northish.
3	1 Day's Walk Southish.
4	2 Day's Walk Southish.
5	3 Day's Walk Eastish.
6	3 Day's Walk Westish.

If instead of looking for the next village, characters simply travel in a particular direction and assume it's 1d6 Day(s) of walking that way.

What's the Village Population?

Dimetrodon Villages have populations of 3d6+1.

Thrinaxodon and **Broomistega** Villages have populations of 1d6x10. If only 10 folks are indicated, assume this is a traditional, unintegrated family unit of either **Thrinaxodons** OR **Broomistegas**, so subtract 1d6 from the population of 10.

D6	WHAT DO FOLKS DO IN THIS VILLAGE?
1-2	Get Food (Hunt, Scavenge and/or Farm).
3	Get Food, Visiting Ulemosaur Merchant.
4	Get Food, Artists/Crafters.
5	Get Food, Artists/Crafters, Education/Training.
6	All of the Above.

D6	DIMETRODON, SPHENACODON, EDAPHOSAURUS ARCHITECTURAL PARTICULARITIES
1-2	The local sunning spot is a patch of exposed dark bedrock with a light-colored stone wall, using dried mud for mortar. The evening side serves as both a stage and a convenient place to stargaze.
3-4	The local sunning spot is floored by a mosaic of colored stones. A convenient boulder serves as a reflecting wall.
5-6	Sunning spot on raised wooden stage, lashed wooden wall.

D6	SECODONTOSAURUS ARCHITECTURAL PARTICULARITIES
1-2	The sunning beach has a flagstone ramp leading into/out from the water, and the shore is protected from erosion by fine gravel gathered from further up/downstream.
3-4	Sand sunning beach, nearby droopy coniferous trees sometimes serve as shelter.
5-6	River stones are stacked into a sunning/shade wall near the beach.

D6	THRINAXODON AND BROOMISTEGA ARCHITECTURAL PARTICULARITIES
1	Spread out settlement, single chamber burrows atop local hills.
2	Burrows crowded into a single large hill, bead curtain doors.
3	Burrows in 3-4 adjacent hills, thatched lean-to entrances.
4	Burrows in 2 large hills, ornate wooden pavilion entrances.
5	Burrows on top of a hill, entire hilltop under wood-shingled pavilion, wooden planks leading in, tapestry doors.
6	Burrows on the north and south face of the hill, smaller entrances covered by clay tile awnings, carved wooden doors.

•***Thrinaxodons*** living traditionally typically dig simple, 2-chamber burrows into the hillsides.

•***Broomistegas*** living traditionally lash together simple structures from still-living vegetation.

D6	WHAT PROBLEM DOES THIS VILLAGE FACE?
1-2	Nothing really.
3	Large Predators (pg 75) have shown up nearby.
4	Food has become scarce.
5	Leader is missing or unwell.
6	Distrust nearby village: 2-in-6 chance distrusted neighbors are *Secodontosaurs* (pg 88).

D6	LOCAL GEOGRAPHY: DIMETRODON MARSHLAND TERRITORIES
1	*LANDSCAPE:* crumbling shale exposed on hillsides and banks of streams. *FLORA:* soft herbaceous ferns, occasional patch of stubby cycad trees and low coniferous bushes.
2	*LANDSCAPE:* low area, ¾ covered in standing water. *FLORA:* moss, algae and a profusion of horsetail ferns occasionally forming thickets.
3	*LANDSCAPE:* wet soil, infrequent pools of standing water and many sluggish streams. *FLORA:* myriad of flowering grasses with a few lonely scale trees 60-100' tall, soon to drop their seeds and die.
4	*LANDSCAPE:* sandy, well-drained soil, lots of streams. *FLORA:* predominantly flowering grasses with bare patches, small, semi-frequent copses of ginkgo trees and stream beds slick with spring-green algae.
5	*LANDSCAPE:* flat area of intensely saturated, rich black clay studded by the occasional rust-colored sandstone boulder. *FLORA:* algae slicks and the occasional tree-sized ailing sigillaria plant covered in bulbous, dayglo fungal growths.
6	*LANDSCAPE:* 90% covered in 1-5' standing water, numerous islands of raised rocky soil. *FLORA:* thick, almost obscuring growth of ferns in the water and 4-12' coniferous trees on the islands.

D6	LOCAL GEOGRAPHY: THRINAXODON AND BROOMISTEGA ALLIED PROTECTORATES
1	*LANDSCAPE:* well-drained rocky soil with numerous yellow-orange sandstone boulders. *FLORA:* flowering grasses, occasional copse of coniferous trees with long, dangling strap-like leaves.
2	*LANDSCAPE:* gently rolling hillocks, infrequent stony rivers and streams. *FLORA:* flowering grasses, largish areas covered by low-growing coniferous bushes.
3	*LANDSCAPE:* rocky and flat, dry other than the rare river or stream. *FLORA:* pale electric-green lichen, stiff short grasses.
4	*LANDSCAPE:* rocky and dry, low rolling hills, plentiful streams. *FLORA:* thin coniferous forest.
5	*LANDSCAPE:* dense damp clay soil, mostly flat. *FLORA:* lush with various wild flowers.
6	*LANDSCAPE:* odd, low undulated ridges. *FLORA:* thick, soft, tall spring-green grass.

NOTE: There are 2 seasons: WET and DRY. The mixed-weather transitory periods when one season wanes and the other waxes are quite long (9-11 months), whereas the seasons themselves are somewhat short (2-4 months). The weather built into the various Encounter Charts, the descriptions in the Local Geography Charts, etc. assume things are happening in either of these transitory periods.

During the WET SEASON it rains heavily, almost everyday. During the cloudless DRY SEASON already warm temps rise drastically, relentlessly baking everything. Most campaigns in this Sphere could take place entirely within one of the transitory periods; however, the fierceness of the seasons and the challenges they bring could make for a dramatic, adventure-hook-filled span of make-believe time.

Village Names can be quickly
improvised in a couple of different ways.

•Roll on the General Names Chart (pg 102) and combine that result with something referencing the local Geography or the Architectural Peculiarities.

•Roll on the General OR Species Name Chart, make that result a part of all the Local NPCs' names and add Village, Settlement, Camp, Town, Gathering, Burrow, Dig, Place, Shores, Beach etc. as appropriate.

And here are a few village names to get you started:

D6	DIMETRODON MARSHLAND TERRITORIES
1	*Old Camp Yellowsail.*
2	*Conefall Village.*
3	*Shawltown.*
4	*The Village by Flower Stream.*
5	*Greater Gal Pals Commune.*
6	*Warm-Fern Township.*

D6	THRINAXODON AND BROOMISTEGA ALLIED PROTECTORATES
1	*The Pretty-Dig.*
2	*Thoughtful Burrows.*
3	*Fuzztree-Thicket Village.*
4	*Needleleaf Place.*
5	*Experiment-Town.*
6	*The Southern Gal Pals Village Cooperative.*

D6	AMMONITE NORTHERN BEACH COMMUNITIES
1	*Sandbeach City.*
2	*Port Question.*
3	*Spiral's Rest.*
4	*Squishy Fish Shoals.*
5	*Dry Swim Village.*
6	*Charmwhirl Cove.*

What about Xenacanthus Schools?

Given their nomadic nature, the presence of a **Xenacanthus** School is indicated by the Xenacanthus Wide River Queendom Encounter Chart (pg 74). Each School has a population of 4d6 souls.

What about Nautiloid Schools?

There are currently 9 colleges/universities in the Marine Conservancy, each marked on the map below. Each has a population of 3d6×100 at any given time; folks come and go between the Schools as they please.

	SCHOOLS OF THE MARINE CONSERVANCY
1	*College of Applied Philosophy.* **Chancellor Hope Wonderfoam,** wistful stargazer.
2	*College of Natural History.* **Chancellor Fizzywhistle Glittersea,** exuberant lecturer.
3	*College of Natural Philosophy.* **Chancellor Budleaf Twinklebright,** forgetful optimist.
4	*College of Hydrological and Thaumaturgical Dynamics.* **Chancellor Kelpy Seastar,** grouchy protector.
5	*Pelagic Pumicefloat University.* **Chancellor Tinselled Prettysweet,** implicitly trustful.
6	*College of Sigils and Semiology.* **Chancellor Saltysail Cleverwits,** gregarious expert.
7	*Shelfside Deepwater University.* **Chancellor Obsidian Largepaw,** benevolent guru.
8	*College of Bringing and Binding.* **Chancellor Sunset Picklebrine,** nurturing provider.
9	*Sootvent Kissing Tubes University of Wizardry.* **Chancellor Glamour Glowbeam,** debonair fashionista.

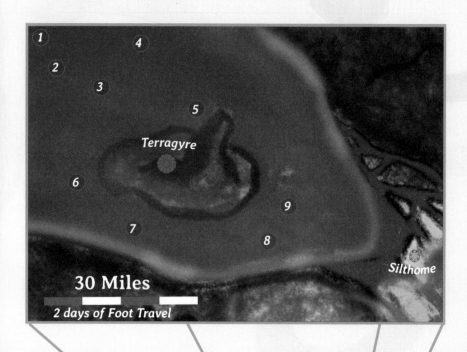

1
4
2
3
5
Terragyre
6
9
7
8
Silthome

30 Miles

2 days of Foot Travel

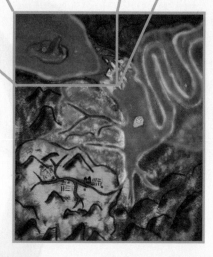

D6	So you chit-chat with the staff of the Busted Barge about Interesting Things in Terragyre
1	For the past year folks have been seeing large orbs of swirling shadows heading towards *Dimetrodon Marshland Territories* around dawn each night of the New Moon. *The Truth:* if followed, these 1d6 Cold Shadow Tangles are headed towards Adventure 2, Part 1 (pg 48).
2	Rumor has it, amongst the few off-world regulars, an entrance to a positively ancient wing of the *Goblin Labyrinth* can be found in one of the basements in town. Students have made a game of thoroughly exploring and mapping the basements at night, looking for this legendary entrance. The ones already explored are marked with an "X" in chalk above the door. *W*: ?????
3	The coral on the southern side of the island has been losing its color! (and thus symbiotic photosynthesizers can't efficiently photosynthesize!). Protests by local Bembexias (pg 78) and Jannasas (pg 85) have been occurring in front of the college on a weekly basis, aided by a few sympathetic wizardry students. The protesters suspect it's runoff from the alchemical studies class. Dean Longshell has investigated on their behalf but found no evidence of the Wizardry College causing the malady, despite a week meticulously observing the School's wastewater system. The protesters plan to postpone until the "Human's Attack!!!" crisis is taken care of. *The Truth*: on the last day of each alchemical class the students make a *Potion of Overwritten Color* as a fun final project. The discarded reagents from that single day of class are causing the coral to lose color, a lesson repeated every 2-3 months. The excitable Janassa fish, **Party Colors**, is the driving force behind the ongoing protests. She does not like **Dean Longshell**.

D6	SO YOU CHIT-CHAT WITH THE STAFF OF THE BUSTED BARGE ABOUT INTERESTING THINGS IN TERRAGYRE
4	Rumor has it a **Giant Ammonite** named **Spiral Precious** has discovered a process which turns sand into gold! *THE TRUTH*: they sort of did. They can turn sand into silver. However, the sand must be processed into very fine glass first. Precious is currently only able to make very small quantities of glass at a time. What they need are several large dense stones, a few hundred pounds of clay and as much charcoal as **Swift Chill** (pg 99) can spare. The process is labor intensive and requires a full lunar cycle. The final products are overwrought with exquisite floral touches. If they're going to do it, **Spiral Precious** intends to do it beautifully.
5	Somebody said the other day, and no creature can remember who, but someone said that ACANTHODES SHARK'S VENOM (pg 76) is useful as a "general anesthetic" if carefully administered, whatever that means. *THE TRUTH*: it's true!
6	The Staff at the *Busted Barge* overheard one of the off-world wizardy students tell another that she had summoned an imp in the attic and trapped him in a jar! *THE TRUTH*: she totally did! There's a trapdoor on the ceiling in the Center of the *Wizardry College*, where the 4 wings meet, but no ladder. The attic itself runs for most of the length and width of the entire School. It's mostly empty except for the occasional crate of emergency rations or sack of odd thaumaturgical supplies. The imp is in a jar at the far end of the westerly wing. **Tlktlkcolona-taboool** (**Tabs** for short) [SKLL:**8** STAM:**6** INIT:**2** ARMR:**0** FLIGHT], looks like a black snake with a rooster's head and fluffy white wings. When outside the jar he can throw very minor curses around at will, 1 curse per soul (e.g. remove a single word from someone's vocabulary forever, permanently reduce Luck by 1d6, and that sort of thing). He can also disappear back to some hell or another by sneezing. Yes, if you trick him into sneezing... season to taste with pepper. You get the idea.

Encounter Charts (roll 1/day)

D6	NAUTILOID AND AMMONITE MARINE CONSERVANCY ENCOUNTER CHART
1	Nothing but sunshine, a soft humid breeze and warm gentle currents.
2	Short, steamy rainstorm then more sunshine.
3	School of ACCANTHODE SPINY SHARKS (PG 76).
4	*Ammonite* wanderer *(pg 76)*.
5	*Nautiloid* Academic or Wizard *(pg 85)*.
6	1d6 HELICOPRION SHARK(S). If alone it's a **HUGE** HELICOPRION (PG 83).

D6	THRINAXODON & BROOMISTEGA ALLIED PROTECTORATES ENCOUNTER CHART
1	Nothing but sunshine and a soft humid breeze.
2	Short, steamy rainstorm then more sunshine.
3	*Thrinaxodon* Lizard Keeper with 4d6 Lizards *(pg 91)*.
4	1d6 *Scutosaurs (pg 87)*.
5	1d6 *Broomistega*, *Thrinaxodon* or *Ulemosaur* wanderers.
6	2d6 *Inostrancevias (pg 84)*.

D6	XENACANTHUS WIDE RIVER QUEENDOM
1	Nothing but sunshine, a soft humid breeze and warm gentle currents.
2	Short, steamy rainstorm then more sunshine.
3	School of 4d6 *Xenacanths (pg 95)*.
4	*Ulemosaur (pg 92)* Boat Trader.
5	1d3 *Estemmenosuchus (pg 81)*.
6	*Uranocentradon (pg 93)*.

D6	DIMETRODON MARSHLAND TERRITORIES
1	Nothing but sunshine and a soft humid breeze.
2	Short, steamy rainstorm then more sunshine.
3	1d6 *Edaphosaurs (pg 80)*.
4	1d6 *Sphenecadons (pg 90)*.
5	1d6 *Secodontosaurs (pg 88)*.
6	WETGRASS HAGBEAST (PG 76).

D6	LARGE PREDATOR CHART
1	ANTEOSAURUS (PG 77).
2	SAUROCTONUS (PG 87).
3	INOSTRANCEVIA (PG 84).
4	RUBIDGEA (PG 86).
5	URANCENTRADON (PG 93).
6	*Estemmenosuchus (pg 81)* (not actually a predator).

D6	HUMAN TERRITORY ENCOUNTER CHART
1	1d3 farmers carrying baskets of produce to *Fort Deadfin*.
2	1d6 children playing dangerously close to a snoring URANOCENTRODON.
3	A pair of loggers bickering over where to begin CUTTING A TREE.
4	Prominent biologist *Znedzy Tartakov,* cataloging therapsids, lost.
5	2D6 'SOLDIERS' (conscripted porters) begrudgingly practicing combat.
6	Nothing but sunshine and a soft humid breeze.

Critter Catalog

Acanthodes Shark

SKILL 6
STAMINA 4
INITIATIVE 2
ARMOUR 0
DAMAGE as Small Beast

MIEN	
1	Cheerful
2	Distracted
3	Chatty
4	Tired
5	Bored
6	Sad

Small, silver, swift filter-feeding marine sharks with a spine on each of their fins. Allies and messengers of the Nautiloids. Tend towards impatience and bouts of impulsiveness.

Special

On a successful attack, defender must Test Luck or their Skill is reduced by 1 as they are afflicted by terrible numbness for 2 hours. Additional "doses" of the venom extend the recovery time by 2 hours. At 12+ hours of numbness victims lose consciousness for the duration.

Ammonite

SKILL 9
STAMINA 12
INITIATIVE 2
ARMOUR 2
DAMAGE as Club

MIEN	
1	Curious
2	Frustrated
3	Haunted
4	Distant
5	Contemplative
6	Bubbly

Very big, spiral shelled marine/terrestrial molluscs with 5 broad, muscular and vibrantly hued tentacles. Each section of their dense, multicolored shells is marked by heavy ridges.

There is no **Ammonite** culture. Each awakens alone and fully-grown, somewhere off the continental shelf, troubled by dreams of fire and iron as well as a compulsion to make their way shoreward. Along the way they inevitably run across one of the 9 Nautiloid Schools, and from them learn many things before coming ashore and breathing with unexpected lungs.

Anteosaurus

Skill **8**
Stamina **21**
Initiative **3**
Armour **3**
Damage as **Large Beast**

	Mien
1	Hungry
2	Peckish
3	Unconcerned
4	Basking
5	Contented
6	Ravenous

Huge (16-20' long) carnivorous synapsids with thick, bony skulls. Usually found singly, noted for their tendency to talkitively luxuriate in an almost beatific, semi-aquatic way... until they get hungry. Then it's sudden, brutal force, gorging, giggles and a nice long nap.

Bembexia

SKILL 2
STAMINA 2
INITIATIVE 1
ARMOUR 1
DAMAGE 1 on a roll of 6+

MIEN	
1	Chatty
2	Very Chatty
3	Talkative
4	Hungry...for Conversation
5	Dejected
6	Terse

Smallish, herbivorous sea snails with marigold to pale orange shells and scarlet feet. Gregarious, loquacious and generally naive.

Broomistega

SKILL 6
STAMINA 5
INITIATIVE 2
ARMOUR 0
DAMAGE as Unarmed

MIEN	
1	Curious
2	Unobservant
3	Cautiously Cordial
4	Effusive
5	Gregarious
6	Quiet

Smallish, brightly colored amphibians with long, broad snouts, cosmopolitan distribution and an even more cosmopolitan attitude. These little ones are everywhere: everywhere there's fresh water and somewhere to hide from bigger, meaner things.

Further, they've developed mutually beneficial relationships with all manner of unexpected species, most famously *Thrinaxodons*.

Cold Shadow Tangles

Skill 7
Stamina 6
Initiative 2
Armour 0
Damage as Special

Their mien is deeply inconsistent and seems to be solely associated with their purpose, as dictated by distant and inscrutable stars.

Writhing masses of darkness around the size of a big barrel, these are clumsy agents of the less indifferent stars. They're rumored to emerge from the deepest depths of the oceanic abyss, making their way landward to whatever purpose the stars intend. Cold Shadow Tangles are rendered immobile and invisible by sunlight; however, their terrible touch remains in effect.

Cold Shadow Tangles can only be harmed by natural attacks from living things. This of course causes the attacker to suffer their terrible touch. Weapons and magic just slip right through them.

Special

D6	Rather than Damage, touching or being touched by Cold Shadow Tangles results in the following:
1	Lose 1 Luck.
2	Lose 2 Luck.
3	Lose 1 Skill for 1 Hour (at 0 Skill lose conciousness).
4	Lose 2 Skill for 1 day (at 0 skill lose consciousness).
5	Become a completely incorporeal shadow for 1d6 hours.
6	Death... no, Undeath. Gain 1d6 Stamina as pain and bleeding no longer matter. You no longer regain Stamina or Luck.

Also, they can only be harmed by natural attacks from living things.

Dimetrodon

SKILL 8
STAMINA 7
INITIATIVE 2
ARMOUR 0
DAMAGE as Modest Beast

	MIEN
1	Big Mood ☹
2	Big Mood ☺
3	Sassy
4	Coy
5	Blunt
6	Exuberant

4'-6' long quadrapedal synapsids with smooth, thick, hairless skin and a spiny sail down their back. Capable of using forelimbs as hands and arms, but only while awkwardly balancing on their tail. *Dimetrodons* mostly come in cool pastel colors, often offset with a pale magenta or sunset orange.

However, *Dimetrodons* tend to take their appearance into their own claws. Self expression is the highest value, the very point of being for some synapsids. Polished stone accessories, claw-knit fabrics and especially flowers are hugely popular.

Edaphosaurus

SKILL 7
STAMINA 9
INITIATIVE 2
ARMOUR 0
DAMAGE as Small Beast

	MIEN
1	Tired
2	Sarcastic
3	Go. Away.
4	Begrudgingly Helpful
5	Surly
6	Saccharine but Genuine

Large, somewhat lumbersome, barrel-chested sail-backed synapsids forever gnawing on leaves, moss and the like. Notable for both the surly nobs on their spines and their typically surly-to-sarcastic disposition.

Eosaurichthys

SKILL 6
STAMINA 6
INITIATIVE 2
ARMOUR 0
DAMAGE as Modest Beast

	MIEN
1	Mean
2	Cruel
3	Amused
4	Aggressive
5	Starving
6	Also Cruel

3' long, seafoam green predatory fish with large powerful fins on their back end and huge toothy jaws on the other. They tend to wait in ambush, hidden amongst the coral. Sometimes these vicious fishes trick the younger, weaker members of the School into attacking larger prey alone while everyone else watches and sniggers in hiding. They usually swim in Schools of 3d6.

Estemmenosuchus

SKILL 9
STAMINA 18
INITIATIVE 3
ARMOUR 1
DAMAGE as Large Beast

	MIEN
1	Oblivious
2	Unaware
3	Almost Insensate
4	Inquisitive
5	Gushy
6	Nonplussed

Huge, semi-aquatic herbivorous therapsids with crowns of knobby horns. They tend to wallow in deepish ponds and streams, obliviously lost in their own bubbling thoughts. They don't mean to be rude, but it takes a minute to get their attention.

Eunotosaurus

SKILL 3
STAMINA 5
INITIATIVE 1
ARMOUR 0
DAMAGE as Small Beast

MIEN	
1	Reluctant
2	Undecided
3	Eager but still Slow
4	Ambivalent
5	Sheepish
6	Daring

These small, turtle-like reptiles lack external shells, though their ribs form a sort of internal, protective shell. The trade off being: it stiffens their movement, slowing them considerably. Though incapable of speech, those interacting with them consider Eunotosaurs to be self-aware and intelligent.

Eurypterid

SKILL 7
STAMINA 8
INITIATIVE 2
ARMOUR 1
DAMAGE as Small Beast

MIEN	
1	Shy
2	Reserved
3	Awkwardly Friendly
4	Nervous
5	Timid
6	Braggadocio

Largeish (4-5'), red-brown, flat-bodied freshwater arthropods with comb-like raking limbs, Eurypterids dwell in the murky bottoms of the Wide River. There they rake through the substrate for tasty gastropod morsels, setting aside the tougher bivalves and brachiopods for their *Xenacanthus* friends. Most are friendly, if a little shy and self-effacing around new folks. If need be Eurypterids can walk short distances across dry land.

Giant Dragonfly

SKILL 6
STAMINA 3
INITIATIVE 3
ARMOUR 0
DAMAGE as Small Beast

MIEN	
1	Hungry
2	Ornery
3	Hungry
4	Ornery
5	Hungry
6	Bored

Raven sized, semi-intelligent dragon flies. They're often kept as pets but can be difficult to handle if they get the least bit hungry. They're usually hungry. They're the largest thing in the skies and have a nasty bite when upset.

Helicoprion

SKILL 8/10
STAMINA 11/24
INITIATIVE 3/2
ARMOUR 0
DAMAGE as Modest/Large Beast

	MIEN
1	Aggressive
2	Hungry
3	Starving
4	Famished
5	Violent
6	Torporous

Mostly mid-sized sharks (3-6' long) with a saw-blade-like toothwhorl on their bottom jaw. Unintelligent and aggressive against weak seeming prey. If only one Helicoprion shark is indicated by an encounter chart it is of the Huge (35') variety. They attack by slashing prey with their bottom jaw, and swallow the resultant chunks whole.

Inostrancevia

Skill 9
Stamina 16
Initiative 3
Armour 0
Damage as Large Beast

	Mien
1	Jeering
2	Napping
3	Ravenous
4	Pissy
5	Mean
6	Vicious

Large (11' long), rusty-orange fur covered, saber-toothed therapsid carnivores, they tend to hunt in small, chortling familial packs of 2d6 adults with 2d6 kits hiding nearby. Noted mostly for their mocking words and hunger-fueled bloodlusts, most creatures try to stay as far away as possible.

Though Inostrancevia's densely muscled form is capable of terrifying speeds, they have very little endurance, thank the stars...

Janassa

Skill 3
Stamina 4
Initiative 2
Armour 0
Damage as Unarmed

Mien	
1	Startled
2	Shocked
3	Alarmed
4	Panicked
5	Cautious
6	Brave

Flat, lobed, skate-like cartilaginous fish who tend to stick close to sandy substrates. They bury their rainbow-colored bodies into the sand as a reaction to ANY surprise. Janassas tend to become chatty and eager to please once they've gotten over the initial shock of meeting anyone new. They voraciously eat small bivalves and brachiopods.

Special
2 Stealth.

Nautiloid

Skill 8
Stamina 5
Initiative 3
Armour 0
Damage as Unarmed

Mien	
1	Aloof
2	Inquisitive
3	Curious
4	Bombastic
5	Bashful
6	Arrogant

Shelled marine molluscs around the size of a large HUMAN head. Some have conical shells while others possess the more familiar whorly-type shells. They're often colored in oceanic blues with dayglow pink, orange and yellow. From the bottom half of their faces sprout dozens of delicate tentacles. They live in long, shallow bays into which the Wide River drains.

Nautiloids gather into literal Schools in great underwater Academic Arenas. There they learn and debate magic, mathmology, natural history, hydrodynamics, etc.

Special
1d6-1 randomly determined Spells.

Levitation.

Telekinesis.

Rubidgea

SKILL 10
STAMINA 21
INITIATIVE 4
ARMOUR 1
DAMAGE as Large Beast

	MIEN
1	Peckish
2	Hungry
3	Starving
4	Chatty
5	Gossipy
6	Napping

As solitary ambush predators these big (11' long) therapsids tend to spend an inordinate amount of time alone. They're often positively cormorous for conversation. They ruthlessly pursue chit-chat the way a hungry dog desperately savages marrow from an old bone. It's deeply unfortunate they only talk about the puerile and inane.

Most Rubidgea prefer to eat things that don't talk back, but their stomachs can certainly screech louder than their prey. Some conversations end in screaming and are followed by a nice long nap.

Sauroctonus

SKILL 10
STAMINA 21
INITIATIVE 4
ARMOUR 1
DAMAGE as Large Beast

	MIEN
1	Sniping
2	Deferent
3	Acquiescent
4	Pompous
5	Blathering
6	Impatient

Large (7'), carnivorous therapsids with pronounced canines and oddly polite dispositions. Solitary, wandering hunters who enjoy getting to know their prey before savagely attacking. Not only does the long wind-up allow a Sauroctonus to gauge their preys' strengths and weaknesses, it's something to pass the time. Boredom tends to drive these big, well-groomed predators as much as hunger. They're one of the few critters that wander between the river valley and the arid uplands.

Special
4-in-6 chance the Sauroctonus slips a parapraxis or two, insinuating the characters are soon to be food. "Nice to eat you! Sorry, meet you. Many apologies..." or "You look just, positively delicious, madam."

Scutosaurus

SKILL 6
STAMINA 16
INITIATIVE 1
ARMOUR 3
DAMAGE as Club

	MIEN
1	Oblivious
2	Unconcerned
3	Cautious
4	Annoyed
5	Quietly Inquisitive
6	Observant

Huge, heavily-muscled grazing reptiles protected by thick bony plates underneath their already tough skin. Scutosaurs never stop wandering, and are constantly chewing. Often considered mute or unintelligent, mostly these cumbersome folks just don't want to talk. "About as chatty as a Scutosaurus" is a classic way to tell someone they're being too quiet. Scutosaurs are found mostly in the dryer, hillier portions of the *Thrinaxodon and Broomistega Allied Protectorates* as well as the arid uplands.

Special
When surprised or hurt, Scutosaurs let out a hugely loud bellow. Test Luck/Skill or be stunned until the end of round.

Secodontosaurus

SKILL 6
STAMINA 7
INITIATIVE 3
ARMOUR 0
DAMAGE as Modest Beast

	MIEN
1	50% Mawkish, 50% Sarcastic
2	Alert
3	Suspicious
4	Napping
5	Irritated
6	Warily Amiable

Semi-aquatic, sail-backed synapsids with a narrow, crocodile-like snout. Tend to hunt much smaller, slower prey in the streams they inhabit. Secodontosaurs endure a mostly unearned reputation for duplicity and viciousness. Still there remain enough bad actors and exaggerated stories that their general reputation isn't likely to change.

They go a little wild when they get angry, and bite and thrash about like mad.

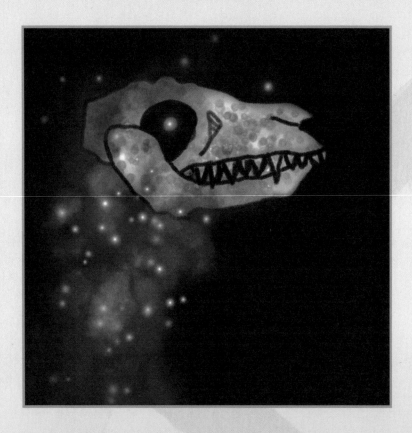

Shame Ghosts of the Friendless Dead

SKILL 10
STAMINA 5
INITIATIVE 1
ARMOUR 2
DAMAGE as Cold Fire of Shame

MIEN*	
1	50% Mawkish, 50% Sarcastic
2	Alert
3	Suspicious
4	Napping
5	Irritated
6	Warily Amiable

DAMAGE ROLL➜	1	2	3	4	5	6	7+
Cold Fire of Shame	3	5	7	9	11	13	21

For the past seventeen years those dying of illness in *Shadepool*, alone and without love, have leapt from their death beds and ran into the night, compelled to die in *Wonder Claw's Dig*. There they fitfully sleep until they rot to only bones. Their skulls then arise each night to pitifully moan, each alone in their presumably eternal torment.

Special

SHAME GHOSTS want, more than anything, a friendly embrace. If expressly denied a hug they attack. If diverted or delayed, there's 10-20 minute window before they MUST know an answer (perhaps 30 minutes if tactfully handled).

D3	IF ALLOWED TO HUG A CHARACTER:
1	Character immediately loses 1d6 Stamina. The screaming cold of the abandoned dead is extremely unhealthy for the living to accept.
2	For the next minute the embrace can be ended. This is how long it takes the skull to embed into someone, after which the Stamina loss becomes permanent. Removed skulls immediately attack.
3	Character gains 1 Armour from the permanent, protective embrace. An ethereal, azure fog hangs about them from dusk until dawn.

Should anyone suggest the ghosts hug each other, seeing as they have so much in common, they most certainly will. This renders them once again inert, lifeless skulls.

---

* These are just a starting point. The Friendless Dead "match energy."

Sphenecadon

SKILL 8
STAMINA 7
INITIATIVE 2
ARMOUR 0
DAMAGE as Modest Beast

	MIEN
1	Friendly
2	Kindly
3	Congenial
4	Vexed
5	Disagreeable
6	Hostile

Swamp dwelling synapsids with short sails, who weave among the frequent ginkgo and scale-tree copses of the **Dimetrodon** territories. Unless raising children, Sphenecadons typically live in idiosyncratic solitude. Famously, all Sphenecadons can speak to the stars, and the stars always listen. This doesn't mean that the stars at all care. The most mystically inclined Sphenecadons can actually hear the stars as they sassily respond.

Special

1-in-6 chance an individual Sphenecadon is a Star Witch. In groups of more than four, a **Star Witch** is present.

Star Witches sacrifice 1d6 years of their life to cast Spells. A given **Star Witch** has 4d6 years remaining.

Roll 1d6 to determine Spells.

1	Call the Voidstar Constellation (pg 26), Light
2	Call the Voidstar Constellation (pg 26), Fear, Flash
3	Constellation Ferocior (pg 26), Constellation of Vitality (pg 26), Invisibility
4	Constellation of Vitality (pg 26), Posthumus Vitality, Peace
5	Constellation of Vitality (pg 26), Jolt
6	Call the Voidstar Constellation (pg 26), Fire Bolt

Thrinaxodon

SKILL 8
STAMINA 6
INITIATIVE 2
ARMOUR 0
DAMAGE as Weapon

MIEN	
1	Inquistive
2	Nosy
3	Welcoming
4	Exuberant
5	Gloomy
6	Dissatisfied

Smallish, sociable, burrowing therapsids with sharp digging claws and pale green fur, glowing softly in the dark. Their burrows are elaborate, highly decorated and often shared with other creatures, especially **Broomistega** Amphibians. **Thrinaxodons** have a particularly easy time standing up, and their hands are usually quite deft.

Thrinaxodons, with the aid of **Broomistegas**, often practice aquaculture, keeping Schools of boneless fish in flooded chthonic chambers. Some **Thrinaxodons** keep herds of lizards amongst the expanding grasslands in their territories. Still others hunt insects, catch fish and aestivate during dry spells, in harmony with the old ways.

Trilobite

SKILL -1
STAMINA 0.1
INITIATIVE 0
ARMOUR -1
DAMAGE as Gentle Caress

MIEN	
1	Trilobite
2	Trilobite
3	Trilobite
4	Trilobite
5	Trilobite?
6	Trilobite!

Very small, flat-bodied arthropods who tend to move in swarms across the ocean floor. Each body segment is a rich, royal blue at the center, fading to soft azure around the edges, all speckled with gold-like glitter.

Triops

SKILL -1
STAMINA 0.1
INITIATIVE 0
ARMOUR -2
DAMAGE as Gentle Caress

MIEN	
1	Swim
2	Eat
3	Swim
4	Eat
5	Swim
6	Eat

Tiny, short-lived, orange crustaceans with shovel-like three-eyed heads and long tails. Varieties live in both freshwater and marine environments.

Ulemosaurus

SKILL 7
STAMINA 11
INITIATIVE 2
ARMOUR 2
DAMAGE as Maul

MIEN	
1	Ponderous
2	Pondering
3	Disquisitive
4	Long-winded
5	Pensive
6	Grumpy

These cumbersome, herbivorous, quadrupedal synapsids don't maintain territories. Rather, they lumber about looking for tasty conifers to eat and new experiences to pursue. A steady diet of piney shrubs gifts their blue-green skin with a deeply resinous scent.

By long tradition, whenever two *Ulemosaurs* meet in their wanderings, they exchange stories and attempt to see if they might be compatible mates. The ritual is the same regardless of gender or the seriousness of either party. Family units tend to homestead near to wherever it was the parents met, just long enough to take their children into adulthood. Though it isn't exactly rare to see an Ulemosaur settled into village life, their reputation as wanderers is well earned.

Finally, all *Ulemosaurs* have 4-5' thick skulls. This combined with their huge size and great strength gives their headbutt devastating effect.

Uranocentrodon

SKILL 13
STAMINA 33
INITIATIVE 3
ARMOUR 3
DAMAGE as Gigantic Beast

	MIEN
1	Sleeping
2	Sleeping
3	Sleeping
4	Sleeping
5	Stirring Slightly
6	Awakening

The Uranocentrodon Amphibians of the Wide River grow especially gigantic (20-30'). Their terrifyingly gigantic mouths are capable of swallowing *Dimetrodons* whole, and even an Anteosaurus in a couple of chomps! Mostly they sleep or sleepingly swim, awakening and eating only rarely.

But, each time one awakens fully, the river froths red with blood and their violent motion.

Wet Grass Hag Beast

SKILL 6
STAMINA 13
INITIATIVE 1
ARMOUR 0
DAMAGE as Weapon or Modest Beast

MIEN	
1	Happy
2	Sad
3	Confused
4	Angry
5	Talkative
6	Kind

Stars pick favorites. Everyone knows this. Living things are idle amusements, and sometimes the stars just aren't done playing when someone dies.

In the dead of a starry night, up through the favored bones of the dead, grow lavender and rose-colored grasses with surprising density. Come the last winking of morning starlight, the Wet Grass Hag Beast awakens with a cyan pinpoint of light where their eyes had been.

After which the creature just goes on about their business, unaware of their change. In fact, they are incapable of comprehending their current state. Sometimes this is days after the creature's death; sometimes it is decades.

Special

Wet Grass Hag Beasts wouldn't do much of anything but a pity; however, interaction (conversation, contact, Spellcasting, etc.) temporarily reduces Skill by 1d3 (successfully Test Luck at Dawn to remove) and PERMANENTLY reduces Luck by 1.

Xenacanthus Shark

SKILL 8
STAMINA 6
INITIATIVE 2
ARMOUR 0
DAMAGE See Special

	MIEN
1	Welcoming
2	Woodenly Polite
3	Mournful
4	Chipper
5	Facetious
6	Blissful

Freshwater shark sporting a poisonous spine projecting backwards from their heads. Azure to pale seafoam green skin bespeckled by sunset hues.

The *Xenacanthus* Sharks live in Schools of extended families, each swearing cooperation to the Brightspine Monarchy and the *ACCORDS*. Below the waterline, alliances and friendships flourish. *Xenacanthus* and Eurypterid folk have long worked together to assure a continued supply of delicious shellfish and aquatic snails all along the Wide River and her many tributaries.

Special

The venom gland of adult *Xenacanths* produces 1d6 stab-doses each day; up to 10 stab-doses can be stored.

DAMAGE ROLL➜	1	2	3	4	5	6	7+
Maddeningly Painful Venom	2	3	4	5	7	13	18

Otherwise the spine does 1 Damage.

Notable NPCs

Queen Sunshine Brightspine, Xenacanthus

SKILL:15 STAMINA:27 INITIATIVE:6 ARMOUR:4 DAMAGE AS GREATSWORD

Ruler of the *Xenacanths*, *Queen Brightspine* has done wondrous things in her 217 year reign. The most notable accomplishment, of course, remains the ACCORDS. She swims amongst her people, holding court wherever she may be. Thus she settles disputes, keeps open the lines of communication with her subjects and recruits new youths to become Accord Keepers.

She suffers terribly from a prophetic dream in which she is killed by HUMAN hands. The poor soul hasn't slept well in decades. She's told no one these dreams, though those close to her are aware she suffers from nightmares.

Her coloration is a rich azure offset by the luscious golden tones of her fins and spine.

ADVANCED SKILLS

1 Meditation

1 Sky Swimming

1 Telekinesis

SPECIAL

Queen Brightspine can instantaneously materialise a huge sword and shield of frozen sunshine under her complete mental control.

Count Joehaund Lizardbane

SKILL:7 STAMINA:7 INITIATIVE:2 ARMOUR:2 DAMAGE AS WEAPON

Count of Lizardbane, "discoverer" of the "Lizard Realm," murderer of critters and second son of DUKE COLDEGRIPPE. He is not well loved. *The Count* has a tendency to cover up his general nervousness and lack of confidence with bombastic boorishness. It's similar to how he covers up his graying hair with black dye. His greatest fear is disappointing his emotionally and physically distant father.

Mayor Budding Stillness, Broomistega

SKILL:**6** STAMINA:**5** INITIATIVE:**2** ARMOUR:**0** DAMAGE AS UNARMED

"I may be small, but I've got big ideas." At 11 inches long, Mayor Budding is short, but that never stopped this restless, chartreuse *Broomistega*. They're working hard to make Shadepool into as inclusive a place as possible. Working right alongside them is their secretary, best friend and life-partner, the *Thrinaxodon* Lumen Cheer.

Dean Longshell, Nautiloid

SKILL:**16** STAMINA:**21** INITIATIVE:**3** ARMOUR:**4** DAMAGE AS FIREBOLT

He has lived for centuries, and intends to live for many more. There is just too much left to understand! A true wizard's work is never finished. *Dean Longshell* is generally at least somewhat anxious about one thing or another. His bumbling academic demeanor can be tossed aside to reveal a quick thinking, decisive leader whensoever an emergency rears its frightful head. *Dean Longshell* hates such periods of crisis, but he tends to handle them well, if at great personal cost.

He spends the first half of every day magically scrying the waterways, worrying over a HUMAN invasion. Afterwards he can usually be found at his wizardly School on *Terragyre*.

His pink and blue shell hasn't grown at all since he was a young man. The shells of *Nautiloids* never stop growing. Eventually the shell becomes large enough to keep them trapped beneath the waves, as their telekinesis can no longer support such bulk. How curious...

SPECIAL

Dean Longshell can cast any Spell that has been created for use with Troika! at will. Rumor has it the Dean has even cast Zed AND made his way back to the point of casting in less than 20 years.

Here are two Spells of his own devising, which he's particularly fond of:

Graven Dictation (1) Carves words spoken aloud by the caster into any flat mineral surface softer than diamonds. Lasts for 10 minutes or until dismissed.

Agelessness (10) Completely halts the aging process. Those blessed by this Spell can still be killed by accident, disease or violence.

Grintooth Wiggles, Dimetrodon

SKILL:9 STAMINA:7 INITIATIVE:2 ARMOUR:0 DAMAGE AS MODEST BEAST

Grintooth has never really been much for fashion, but stays in line with the latest trends thanks to her husband, Warm Flower. She's rather new to her role as Matriarch, and would rather be focused on perfecting the art of dance. Still, when her kin called on her to lead the clan, she accepted the responsibility without question.

Unlike her predecessors, Matriarch Grintooth allows the aggrieved and the accused to speak until they are satisfied. She knows everything she needs to judge their complaint rather than deciding when she knows enough. It's a small change, and it takes much longer; however, even those she's decided against thus far have been content with her decisions.

ADVANCED SKILLS
2 Dancing
1 Constellation of Seeing
1 Etiquette

Softtouch Cuddles, Thrinaxodon

SKILL:8 STAMINA:6 INITIATIVE:2 ARMOUR:0 DAMAGE AS WEAPON

Softtouch Cuddles was cocksure and a bit too impulsive in his youth. A decade ago, all the hair got burnt off his tail in a terrible acid-etching experiment. He's grown quite a lot in the past few years since he took over as village leader, but never really moved past those particular foibles. In fact, just last year he succeeded in etching an intricate design into a copper sheet AND in filling his burrow with dangerously noxious fumes.

Twinkle Eyes, Broomistega

SKILL:9 STAMINA:7 INITIATIVE:2 ARMOUR:0 DAMAGE AS DAGGER

The best **Broomistega** hunter to ever have lived, or so the story goes. If asked she just mutters "Oh, I'm alright, I reckon." Despite getting on in years, Twinkle Eyes still wanders about, looking for new challenges.

Softie Strong, Ulemosaur

SKILL 7 STAMINA 11 INITIATIVE 2 ARMOUR 2 DAMAGE AS MAUL

Ol' Softie's been walking the same road for 15 years now: from **Swift Chill's** forge to the outskirts of *Shadepool* and back again. He carries useful iron items (nails, knives, hinges, saws, chisels, etc.) to dozens of Thrinaxodon and **Broomistega** communities, trading for foodstuffs, textiles and iron ore.

True Bright, Xenacanthus

SKILL:8 STAMINA:6 INITIATIVE:2 ARMOUR:0 DAMAGE AS SPEAR

The albino instructor to the Accord Keepers never strays far from *Gold Stone Island*. True Bright seems to have no funny bone, nor bit of cartilage, in her long, albino pink body. She's kind but very literal. Her particular lance of frozen sunlight has a distinctive hook on one end.

ADVANCED SKILLS
1 Spell — Control Rope

SPECIAL
The venom gland of adult *Xenacanths* produces 1d6 stab-doses each day; up to 10 stab-doses can be stored.

DAMAGE ROLL➜	1	2	3	4	5	6	7+
Maddeningly Painful Venom	2	3	4	5	7	13	18

Otherwise the spine does 1 Damage.

Shelly Elation, Nautiloid

SKILL:8 STAMINA:5 INITIATIVE:3 ARMOUR:0 DAMAGE AS UNARMED

She's been a resident and de facto emergency leader of *Silthome* ever since her's was the only home not washed away by a humongous wave several years ago. She tends to be fairly pragmatic, but often doggedly sticks to whatever idea she has first. Shelly spends most of her time carefully making sand paintings on split pieces of driftwood, using sea life mucilage as glue. She leaves her little stacked stone hut as little as possible.

ADVANCED SKILLS
2 Lungs
1 Levitate
1 Telekinesis

Swift Chill, Ammonite

SKILL:9 STAMINA:12 INITIATIVE:2 ARMOUR:2 DAMAGE AS CLUB

Years pounding away on a forge and breathing charcoal smoke have done Swift Chill's hearing and lungs no favors. He coughs and spits and "What's that you say?" frequently. He spends his days meditatively beating out a rhythm on the forge or making charcoal in the nearby kiln. Evenings are for swimming in the sea. Generally a very obliging soul, he gets rather grumpy with long company at his seaside home on the Protectorate's northern shore.

ADVANCED SKILLS
1 Blacksmithing

1D66	GENERAL NAME INSPIRATION	1D66	GENERAL NAME INSPIRATION
11	Bright, Brightly, Vibrant	41	Joy, Jubilee, Glee
12	Gleam, Gleaming	42	Blush, Glow
13	Soft, Fluffy	43	Bloom, Bud
14	Bold, Brave	44	Fern, Mossy
15	Twinkly, Glitter, Sparkle	45	Leaf, Pineneedle
16	Sunshine, Shining	46	Sunrise, Sunset
21	Happy, Upbeat	51	Elation, Paradise, Bliss
22	Moonglow, Moonbeam	52	Grin, Laugh, Titter
23	Merry, Cheer, Cheerful	53	Flash, Crash, Brash
24	Swift, Quick	54	Dashing, Breezy, Sassy
25	Sweet, Saccharine	55	Pretty, Beautiful, Cutey
26	Bubbles, Fizzy	56	Zippity, Spice
31	Splash, Wave, Rain, Fresh	61	Dapper, Snazzy
32	Singsong,Serenade,Whistle	62	Delight, Charm
33	Flower, Floral, Flora	63	Crystal, Gem, Precious
34	Glimmer, Twinkle	64	Cuddle, Hugs
35	Shimmer, Glowbeam	65	Hope, Wish
36	Shine, Light	66	Wonder, Wander, Daydream

2D6	NAUTILOID & AMMONITE NAME INSPIRATION CHART	2D6	DIMETRODON NAME INSPIRATION CHART
2-3	Ocean, Seas, Blue	2-3	Fashion, Shawl, Gem
4	Seamfoam, Squirt	4	Nibbles, Nip
5	Jet, Scoot	5	Sashay, Wiggle
6	Whorl, Whirl, Long, Tall	6	Sail, Fan
7	Shell, Shelly	7	Warm, Sunbathe
8	Thought, Clever, Wits	8	Glam, Glamour, Fabulous
9	Current, Flow	9	Stars, Fortune, Fickle
10	Coral, Reef	10	Runway, Stage
11-12	Wave, Break, Breaker	11-12	Longtooth